BASKETBALL IN LONG BEACH

BASKETBALL IN LONG BEACH

MIKE GUARDABASCIO & CHRIS TREVINO

Published by The History Press
Charleston, SC 29403
www.historypress.net

Copyright © 2015 by Mike Guardabascio & Chris Trevino
All rights reserved

First published 2015

Manufactured in the United States

ISBN 978.1.60949.975.4

Library of Congress Control Number: 2015940378

Notice: The information in this book is true and complete to the best of our knowledge. It is offered without guarantee on the part of the authors or The History Press. The authors and The History Press disclaim all liability in connection with the use of this book.

All rights reserved. No part of this book may be reproduced or transmitted in any form whatsoever without prior written permission from the publisher except in the case of brief quotations embodied in critical articles and reviews.

For Vincent, my favorite little baller.
—Mike

For Mom, Dad and Tomas, my biggest fans.
—Chris

Contents

Acknowledgements	9
Introduction	13
1. Long Beach State Men	15
2. Long Beach State Women	59
3. Frank Burlison: Long Beach's Basketball Scribe	69
4. Pro Basketball in Long Beach and the Summer Pro League	71
5. Long Beach Poly	79
6. Long Beach City College	117
7. Long Beach Wilson	131
8. Long Beach Jordan	141
9. St. Anthony	149
10. Millikan and Lakewood	157
Index	167
About the Authors	171

Acknowledgements

Though our names are the only ones appearing on the cover, this book is really the collaborative effort of a number of people. Unfortunately, space prohibits us from individually thanking everyone who helped in some way. Please forgive any omissions.

First, our thanks to Jerry Roberts, Will McKay, Megan Laddusaw and the rest of the team at The History Press for their guidance and hard work.

Our gratitude goes to everyone who shared his or her time for an interview. We are especially grateful to Frank Burlison, Ron Palmer, Bill Odell, Tim Sweeney, Joan Bonvicini, John Atkinson, Sharrief Metoyer, Darrick Martin, Lorene Morgan, Jim McCormack, Ed Ratleff, Gary Anderson, Tap Nixon, Dan Monson, Lute Olson and Donna Prindle.

Our thanks go to *Press-Telegram/Gazette*'s photographers Stephen Dachman, William Johnson, Thomas Cordova and Scott Varley, as well as Long Beach's high school yearbook photographers from the last one hundred years for being generous with the art in this book.

From Mike

My thanks go to two of the *Gazette*'s and *Press-Telegram*'s other writers (and two of my best friends), JJ Fiddler and Tyler Hendrickson, for helping pick up the slack during the two years this book was being researched and written.

ACKNOWLEDGEMENTS

Thanks to my mother-in-law, Joyce, for being a willing babysitter and to the administrations of Long Beach State, Jordan, St. Anthony, Millikan, Lakewood and Long Beach Poly for their help. Principals Joe Carlson and Victor Jarels at Long Beach Poly set me up in an office on that campus and gave me space to research for a month. Thanks, once again, to three English teachers there—Judy Haenn, Laura Leaney and Rob Pigott—for helping me find my way.

Thanks go to Brian Walsh at St. Anthony, Lamar Biffle at Jordan, Lorene Morgan at Millikan and Andrea Ohta at Long Beach State for facilitating research and providing temporary office space. Thanks, as well, to my co-author and fellow *Press-Telegram* writer Chris Trevino—he was the shot in the arm this book needed.

And last but not least, thanks to my family. My wife helped give me the time I needed to write this book and the support I needed to see it through. Our toddler, Vincent, makes for a pretty good distraction and already seems to have taken a liking to hoops. My father-in-law, Mits Higa, passed away during the writing of this book—he was an amazing dad and grandfather and a great fan, and he's missed daily.

From Chris

My biggest thanks go to the co-writer of this book, my boss and my friend Mike Guardabascio, for asking me to be a part of this journey and allowing me to accomplish a dream of mine. His guidance and advice meant the world to me during this project.

Thank you to my fellow writers at the *Press-Telegram*, JJ Fiddler and Tyler Hendrickson, for being friends and helpful sources.

A huge thanks to Long Beach State, especially Roger Kirk for all the mornings I spent barging into his office for media guides; to Long Beach Wilson's Jeff Evans and Lia Ladas; and to the Long Beach City College Foundation and the always-helpful Lois Schneider.

While they may be many miles away from me, thank you to all my friends back home in Maryland—too many to name, but thank you for all the encouragement. Special recognition to my unofficial editor since freshman year and one of my closest friends Robert DiMauro for your input on this project. Also thank you to Pauline Ziadeh for all her love and encouragement throughout.

ACKNOWLEDGEMENTS

Of course, a huge thanks to my parents, Lucy and Enrique, my biggest fans, to whom I can always turn for love and support.

And last but not least, thank you to my younger brother, Tomas, for all your support from overseas. Hopefully, you will think about our epic one-on-one basketball games in the driveway when reading this.

INTRODUCTION

Pull open the double doors and step inside, out of the harsh sunlight. The gyms in Long Beach are hot, but at least there's shade and plenty of stories to pass the time. On the walls is the city's history, numbers representing the years gone by. Every gym has a banner, and every banner has a legend—a star player, a thrilling victory, an elated fan base.

The citizens of Long Beach started playing basketball in the early 1900s, just a decade or so after the sport was created in a gymnasium across the country. It took a few years for it to catch on, but once it did, the sport took root and flourished.

While you lace up your sneakers and warm up, we're going to give you a tour of the history of basketball in Long Beach, a history rich with championships and great players.

You'll learn about the tradition of ferocious girls' hoops players, established in the first years of the twentieth century as midwestern migrants brought with them the radical idea that women were capable of working just as hard as men. The daughters of Iowa farmers established a proud precedent of women trailblazers in the city that extended from the early years at Long Beach Poly to the NCAA Final Four teams of Joan Bonvicini at Long Beach State.

From the earliest days, Long Beach was well known for its top-notch coaches. Three former coaches of the Long Beach State men's basketball team—Jerry Tarkanian, Lute Olson and Tex Winter—are enshrined in the Naismith Memorial Hall of Fame in Springfield, Massachusetts, and

INTRODUCTION

men like Ron Palmer and Ron Massey were praised from coast to coast for bringing discipline to the athleticism-rich high school courts of Long Beach Poly and Jordan. That tradition held sway at Long Beach City, as well, where great coaches led the Vikings to many championships.

Their stories and so many more are contained within the pages of this book. As with any exploration of a city with as rich a past as Long Beach, there wasn't room to mention every great team and player. An effort to trace the highlight years of the 49ers and Jackrabbits could easily have filled two books by themselves. We've opted instead to try to include the top teams from each of the city's schools, from the Moore League stalwarts like Poly, Wilson, Jordan, Millikan and Lakewood to St. Anthony and the colleges, Long Beach State and Long Beach City. Special attention has been paid to each school's CIF or state championship teams.

We also take a look at the NBA's Summer Pro League and other professional forays in the area and profile Frank Burlison, the sportswriter who has watched more Long Beach hoops than anyone else.

And remember, just because you finish reading the book doesn't mean you've finished the story. Keep following the local teams in the *Gazette* and the *Press-Telegram*—rarely does a year go by without a Long Beach team claiming a championship.

1
Long Beach State Men

On September 28, 1949, Long Beach State—or as it was known then, Los Angeles–Orange County State College—officially opened its doors in a converted two-story apartment complex off East Anaheim Street in Long Beach. The new college, signed into existence on January of that year by Governor Earl Warren, welcomed 169 students, mainly women and veterans, along with 13 full-time faculty members.

With the booming growth of the population following World War II, a 1947 state survey showed the need for a college to serve the Orange and southeastern Los Angeles area.

Within two decades, the college born out of an apartment complex with a graduating class of just thirty-one students became one of the giants of college basketball with a rich legacy featuring three of the greatest coaches in college basketball history.

The Beginning

Just one year after opening and changing its name to Long Beach State College, Long Beach rolled out its first basketball squad in 1950, with the first practice at Stephens Junior High welcoming sixteen attendees.

The 49ers were led by head coach Herm Schwarzkopf, a former player at Kansas State, who spent time as the coach of Long Beach City College just up the road from 1945 until 1947, marking the first of many City College to Long Beach State connections.

On Saturday, November 18, Long Beach played its first game against Redlands University, a 63–39 loss. Not only was it the program's first basketball game, but it also marked the school's first athletic contest ever.

The 49ers picked up the school's first win in December, a 48–38 victory over Balboa at the National Guard Armory. That inaugural team won just three games in a 3-14 effort that season. Schwarzkopf and the 49ers put together their first double digit total in the 1951–52 season, racking up ten wins against thirteen losses.

Those two seasons would be all for Schwarzkopf, leading the way for Earl Kidd to take the reins of the program for the next several seasons. Kidd is credited with being the first official head coach, hired under the school's first athletic director, Dr. Jack Montgomery, who was lured from UCLA in 1951.

Kidd, a Portland native and World War II veteran, put together the first winning season in Long Beach's young history with a 13-9 mark in 1953, a schedule that pitted the 49ers against the USC freshman squad, the UCLA junior varsity and the Long Beach Air Base.

Kidd led the program for five seasons, adding another winning season in 1954 (13-8) and going out with a 7-20 season in 1957, the first season Long Beach State played in a conference, the California Collegiate Athletic Association (CCAA). The CCAA was founded in 1938, with UC Santa Barbara, Fresno State, San Diego State and San Jose State as the charter members. When the 49ers joined, they went 0-8 in league play.

With Kidd moving on, Bill Patterson, a familiar name in Long Beach after his successful but brief stint at Long Beach Wilson, took over. Patterson coached at John Muir High School in Pasadena in the late 1940s before heading to Wilson in 1951 for five seasons, capturing a league title in 1954. Patterson also spent two years as an assistant coach at Compton Junior College and as the athletic director at Millikan.

But the Patterson years would last just three—a pair of 10-13 seasons and a 17-7 year in 1960, which at the time was the best season in Long Beach State history.

Patterson resigned at the end of the year, citing that he needed more time to work on his doctorate degree.

Long Beach kept the Wilson connection going with its next hire, Richard Perry, a Wilson and College of Emporia graduate. Perry served as an assistant under Patterson and also as a freshman coach on the football team.

BASKETBALL IN LONG BEACH

Earl Kidd was the first official LBSU head coach in program history. Long Beach Press-Telegram *photo archive*.

The Perry years were headlined by a trio of 49ers players: Dave Jones, Bill Florentine and future Olympian John Rambo, the first true stars of Long Beach State basketball.

The six-foot-five rebounding star Jones walked on campus with a considerable amount of hype after helping Long Beach City College to a state championship under head coach Charlie Church. Jones was as advertised, setting the single-season rebounding record, a 13.8 average in the 1960–61 season, which still stands to this day. Florentine proved himself an adept scorer to Jones's rebounding; his 18.9 points-per-game average still ranks number eighteen on the single-season list.

BASKETBALL IN LONG BEACH

But it was Rambo who was a superstar the school had never seen before. Born in Atlanta, Texas, he eventually made his way to Long Beach and starred at Poly in track and basketball.

Rambo headed up to Long Beach City College after graduating, again starring at both sports. He averaged nineteen points per game and also became the first community college high jumper to clear the seven-foot mark.

Local sports fan were excited that Rambo decided to stay in the city, transferring to Long Beach State, where he added to his growing legacy.

Rambo became a 49er during the 1963–64 season, right after the graduation of Jones and Florentine. He was thrown into the star role, along with John Barnicoat, a highly heralded recruit out of Riverside.

The former Jackrabbit Rambo thrived on the court, averaging 19.2 points per game, 9.1 rebounds and a 23.0-point scoring average in conference play.

His legend grew after scoring twenty-seven points in a Friday game against Chapman College; he then high jumped six feet, nine and three-quarters inches the following afternoon and went on to break the single-game scoring record, with forty-two points against the University of San Diego, five hours later.

Rambo outdid that total later in the season with seventy-two points in two games, earning himself Southern California Player of the Week and an All Southland selection.

Rambo's basketball accolades took a backseat to his achievements in track. He won the high jump championship at the NCAAs with a seven-foot-one-and-a-quarter jump in 1964, the best in the nation and best in the world for two months. Then, in the summer, Rambo represented the 49ers and the United States at the 1964 Tokyo Olympics, winning the bronze medal.

It would be hard to return to the court after an offseason like that, but Rambo came back for his final season, making up the "Long John" team of 1964–65 that featured Barnicoat, six-foot-six Johnny Johnson and Carl "the Comet" Washington. While they went an impressive 17-9, the 49ers finished just third in the conference.

Perry coached two more seasons, resigning for a teaching job at USC. Perry's last-minute departure called for an interim coach, won by Randy Sandefur, an assistant for three seasons under Perry, a volleyball and freshman football coach and a three-year varsity winner at Long Beach State in the early 1960s. Sandefur's team fielded a reserve guard from Millikan named Mike Montgomery, who went on to become a well-regarded college coach at Montana and Stanford, leading the latter to the Final Four.

Sandefur spent only one season at Long Beach—a Shark was on its way.

BASKETBALL IN LONG BEACH

Jerry Tarkanian

The biggest catalyst for the rise of not just basketball at Long Beach State but also athletics in general came with the hiring of the school's third athletic director, Dr. Fred Miller, in 1967.

"That's when everything really changed. Long Beach was really known as a teacher's college...but the athletic success for the most part was pretty pedestrian," says longtime *Press-Telegram* sports editor and former Long Beach State beat writer Jim McCormack. "Miller had bigger designs."

Among Miller's first hires were Jim Stangeland, the football coach from Long Beach City College who won three national titles with the Vikings, and Don Gambril, the legendary swim coach and Olympic assistant who led the 49ers to a national title in 1968.

But Miller's hire of a successful junior college coach from Pasadena named Jerry Tarkanian would officially put Long Beach State on the map.

Miller had to take notice of the unprecedented success Tarkanian was having in the junior college ranks, building powerhouses at Riverside City College and Pasadena City College through recruiting—a practice that, at the time, wasn't big at that level.

After playing at Fresno State and coaching at the high school level for several seasons, Riverside came calling for Tarkanian's service, and the Ohio native led the Tigers to three straight state titles in four seasons. Tarkanian, who

Jerry Tarkanian as the head coach of the number one–ranked UNLV Rebels in the PCAA title game (1987). Long Beach Press-Telegram *photo archive.*

BASKETBALL IN LONG BEACH

Head coach Jerry Tarkanian taking in the game from the bench during the 1973 season. Long Beach Press-Telegram *photo archive*.

earned the nickname "Tark the Shark," left for Pasadena in 1967 and won his fourth-straight state crown with a 35-1 record, leaving for Long Beach State after one more season. His overall record in that span was 198-13; an article by *Sports Illustrated* in 1968 dubbed Tarkanian the "Pied Piper of Pasadena."

It was unclear what early expectations Long Beach fans and the administration had for Tarkanian, but the first-year head coach surely surpassed all of them with a 23-3 mark and the program's first conference championship.

That team was built around Tarkanian's first recruit to Long Beach State, Sam Robinson, a standout for Tarkanian at Pasadena who was named the California Junior College Player of the Year.

Robinson was a prep All-American at Jefferson High in Los Angeles and was set on playing for UCLA, but his mother wanted him to stay close to home. While growing up, Robinson was essential to helping the family survive. He worked at a local gas station at the age of twelve; the owner was under the impression that the six-foot-three Robinson was much older.

It didn't take long for Tarkanian to get Robinson to Pasadena and eventually to Long Beach.

BASKETBALL IN LONG BEACH

"My mom liked Tark and so did I," said Robinson. "And the rest was history."

Robinson averaged 19.7 points per game during the finest season in school history. Despite the fact that Long Beach's only losses that season were to Tulsa, an overtime loss to UNLV and a seven-point loss to Fresno State, the 49ers were left at home for the postseason.

"[Tark] told us that he was sorry, that it was because of the NCAA why we didn't go to the NIT [National Invitation Tournament]," remembers Robinson. "It was disappointing."

However, Long Beach could not be denied its first berth in the postseason after the 1970 season. The 49ers finished 24-5 and won the Pacific Coast Athletic Association (PCAA) championship with a 10-0 record and the conference's automatic bid to the NCAA Tournament.

Portrait of Sam Robinson, Jerry Tarkanian's first recruit and a Long Beach State Hall of Fame member. Long Beach Press-Telegram *photo archive*.

Tarkanian's postseason bunch was again built around the six-foot-seven Robinson but got some help from Tarkanian's second-straight California Junior College Player of the Year, the six-foot-eight George Trapp, who had played under Tarkanian at Pasadena as well.

Long Beach won its first tournament game with a 92–73 clobbering of Weber State behind seventeen points from Trapp to advance to the Western Regional semifinals, where it would face John Wooden's UCLA Bruins.

UCLA controlled the game in front of 5,500 fans in Seattle, led by stars Sidney Wicks and Curtis Rowe to an 88–65 win, forcing Long Beach into nineteen turnovers and out-rebounding the 49ers by twenty. Trapp and Robinson combined for thirty-eight points.

Long Beach's historic season came to an end in an 89–86 loss to Santa Clara in the third-place game as future Philadelphia 76er Dennis Awtrey scored thirty-seven points on fifteen-for-seventeen shooting; the 49ers finished the season ranked number fifteen in the nation.

BASKETBALL IN LONG BEACH

George Trapp, number thirty, right before the tip-off. *Long Beach Press-Telegram photo archive.*

It was natural, after the successful season, for the fans' expectations to continue to grow. But the 49ers would need to find a replacement for Robinson, who became the first Long Beach State athlete to be drafted by a professional team—the American Basketball Association's Miami Floridians drafted him in the first round. Robinson also became the program's first All-American, while Trapp was named the conference player of the year.

While the loss of Robinson was monumental, Long Beach fans were ready for their next big superstar: Ed Ratleff.

BASKETBALL IN LONG BEACH

Ed Ratleff

In Ohio prep basketball history, there are few who could match the career of Ed Ratleff. Born in Bellefontaine, Ohio, home of the first concrete street in America, and raised in Columbus, Ratleff became a local legend through basketball. He led Columbus East High School to two state titles, finishing with a 70-1 career record, never losing a home game.

Of course, Ratleff's first love growing up was baseball. And in seventh grade, when his baseball coach, who coincidentally was also the basketball

Ed Ratleff goes for a layup. Long Beach Press-Telegram *photo archive*.

coach, put him on the junior high school basketball team, there was no instant stardom.

"I didn't play unless we were thirty points up," says Ratleff with a laugh.

As last man on the bench, Ratleff was friends with the team's star player, a ninth grader (ninth grade was still considered junior high at this time) by the name of Vance Carr.

Naturally, as the best player on the team, Carr was one of the most popular kids in school; in fact, he was officially *the* most popular after being named Court King of the school—essentially homecoming king—that year. Oddly enough, Carr being named king of junior high would pave the way for Long Beach State's greatest basketball player.

"I figured if I became a really good player, I can become the Court King in junior high and maybe I can get a girlfriend," recalls Ratleff.

In pursuit of this goal, Ratleff dedicated himself to becoming the best player in junior high after that forgettable first season. The newly motivated Ratleff played both basketball and baseball every single day for the entire summer. These were the days before Amateur Athletic Union (AAU) and travel ball teams in the offseason, so Ratleff's games were on the blacktops of the city's parks against other locals.

"I got my butt beat a lot," says Ratleff. "But I kept challenging guys back and forth."

Once Ratleff defeated someone he at first could not beat, he would move on to the next opponent and so on. It also helped that Ratleff grew from five-foot-ten to a massive six-four in one summer, bypassing the awkwardness of a new body and maintaining his coordination.

Ratleff was not only the best player in junior high when the eighth grade school year rolled around but also one of the best in the entire region. He eventually became one of the best in Ohio—and the nation—after leading East High to state titles in 1968 and '69.

By the time Ratleff's senior year came to a close, Ohio State and a majority of the Big 10 schools, along with Florida State, were clamoring for Ratleff's services. The Seminoles were Ratleff's favorite; he nearly committed himself there on a trip, but the Ohio native was put off during his recruiting visit.

Once again, Vance Carr came into play in shaping Ratleff's future.

After graduation, Carr had moved out to Southern California to live with family and attend school. Interested in Pasadena City College, Carr went to check out the campus and came upon Tarkanian, already in the process of heading to Long Beach State, in a hallway.

BASKETBALL IN LONG BEACH

Carr wandered up to the famous coach, introducing himself as an Ohio native and someone interested in the basketball program.

"He looked at me and said, 'Who is better, [future NBA player] Nick Weatherspoon or Eddie Ratleff?'" says Carr. "I said, 'Not even close, Eddie is.'"

Tarkanian was well aware of Ratleff and his accolades in Ohio; he had even placed phone calls to Ratleff, but to no avail. But this time, Carr made the call for Tarkanian, and the coach was finally able to get Ratleff on a plane for a visit.

Long Beach met some of the biggest criteria for Ratleff: it was a place he could live after he graduated, Tarkanian was going to allow him to play baseball and it was not too big. The latter was important, Ratleff remembers, because he didn't think he was really that good.

When Ratleff made it out to the Southland, Tarkanian wasn't putting recruiting pressure on his Ohio visitor, Ratleff recalled.

"He had never seen me play before," said Ratleff. "He didn't know if I was good or not."

That changed after Tarkanian took Ratleff to a pickup game with some of the 49ers and other college players in LA. In Ratleff's mind, it was an unofficial tryout.

"I can't remember how well I played, but I know on the way back in the car he offered me a scholarship about twenty times. So I figured I did OK," says Ratleff with a laugh.

Ratleff ended up committing after the visit, and Tarkanian had another big recruiting score—although the coach needed to survive a late push from Southwest Louisiana State to lock up Ratleff.

While Tarkanian was making history in leading the program to its first NCAA Tournament bid in 1970, Ratleff was busy abusing opponents on the freshman team. As a freshman, the six-foot-six Ratleff averaged a jaw-dropping 39.7 points per game, which led the nation for his class, and 25.4 rebounds per night, all before the three-point line and shot clock were instituted.

Ratleff's highlights were scoring seventy-two points in the first game of the freshman season against Long Beach City College's backup team and putting up sixty-five points in the season finale against San Diego State. Ratleff also scored thirty-five points against the varsity in the inter-squad scrimmage.

"I don't really know how I did it," says Ratleff. "I seriously don't."

After a few games, the freshman head coach, Ivan Duncan, Tarkanian's lead recruiter, called a meeting—a puzzling notion to Ratleff, who said Duncan was not that type of coach.

"He walks in, and he says we have two rules. [Teammate] Roy Miller and I look at each other because we don't have any rules," said Ratleff. "He said,

BASKETBALL IN LONG BEACH

Ed Ratleff trying to get a shot off against a defender. Long Beach Press-Telegram *photo archive.*

BASKETBALL IN LONG BEACH

'Rule number one is pass the ball to Ed. Rule number two is don't forget rule number one.

"It was outrageous. A lot of people would come early to watch me play. I had a lot of flair," says Ratleff. "One magazine called me the black Pete Maravich."

Fans finally got to see the impressive Ratleff and all his flair hit the court for the varsity the following season. The school's basketball program wrote, "People in Long Beach are more excited about Ed Ratleff than any other player in school history."

Ratleff entered the starting lineup that returned the conference player of the year in Trapp and welcomed the third-straight California Junior College Player of the Year in Chuck Terry, from Lute Olson's program at Long Beach City College.

The 49ers got off to a rough start in the season opener against Kansas, falling behind 32–8 at halftime. But something clicked during the game, and the 49ers roared back. The Jayhawks needed to stall to come away with a narrow victory.

"We just kept getting better and better. That was it," says Ratleff. "After that, we started playing…we started gelling together."

Long Beach v. UCLA

Once again, Long Beach rolled to another PCAA title with a 10-0 mark, losing just three more games after that season-opening loss to Kansas—those three losses coming in a four-game span.

Another conference title meant another automatic berth in the NCAA Tournament. The 49ers rolled past Weber State, 77–66, in the first round in Logan, Utah. Ratleff scored thirty-one points and had thirteen rebounds. Long Beach then headed to Salt Lake City to take on Pacific.

The Tigers gave the 49ers problems as Long Beach fell behind 44–31 at halftime, but despite four Pacific players reaching double figures, the 49ers advanced to the Western Regional final behind twenty-three and eighteen points from Trapp and Terry, respectively, in the 78–65 win.

The Pacific win set up a rematch with number one UCLA, and the defending national champions, the Bruins, were looking for their fifth-straight title.

While the Bruins were able to dominate in the previous year's game en route to a twenty-three-point win, it was the 49ers who took control, coming from four points down for a 37–31 lead at halftime.

BASKETBALL IN LONG BEACH

Chuck Terry of Long Beach goes up for a rebound against University of the Pacific in the NCAA Far West Regional. LBSU won 78–65. Long Beach Press-Telegram *photo archive*.

"Trapp and Ratleff," says Glenn McDonald, a freshman on that team and future NBA champion with the Boston Celtics, "they were destroying them."

Tarkanian moved away from his patented 1-1-3 zone defense to a 2-3 zone that "surprised" Wooden; the Bruins struggled to score, falling behind by thirteen points with a little more than fourteen minutes left.

But a three-minute stretch without scoring for Long Beach allowed the defending champs to cut the lead to two points. With their cushion gone, the 49ers were dealt another blow when Ratleff fouled out at the 5:23 mark—the first, and only, time Ratleff fouled out in his college career. It's a foul still heavily reflected on as a controversial call.

BASKETBALL IN LONG BEACH

George Trapp loses the ball during an NCAA game against University of the Pacific as Ed Ratleff watches. *Long Beach Press-Telegram photo archive.*

"We had the game won," says Ratleff. "I think they cheated us."

Legend has it that at halftime, UCLA athletic director J.D. Morgan berated the officials, his Bruins getting all they could handle from the 49ers.

The final turning point of the game was a fourteen-foot jumper taken by Compton native Dwight Taylor, attempted with 2:45 left and the game tied at 53–53. The shot was off, and the Bruins rebounded. Sidney Wicks eventually drew a foul on Taylor with twenty-five seconds left to

BASKETBALL IN LONG BEACH

LBSU v. UCLA in the 1971 West Regional final in Salt Lake City. Long Beach fell 57–55. Long Beach Press-Telegram *photo archive*.

put the Bruins up. Taylor's shot became infamous in Long Beach State history, one Tarkanian wished he had not taken; he would have rather stalled the ball and let the clock wind all the way down for a final shot.

"It was something that haunted Dwight," says McCormack.

Taylor's story came to a tragic end years after that game; the former 49er was shot and killed while walking to buy some milk during the Watts riots.

Wooden told the media that he was sure, when trailing by eleven, that the season was over, already thinking of travel arrangements in place for him and his wife when they lost. But instead, the Bruins went on to win their fifth-straight championship.

"There's no doubt in my mind that if we had beaten UCLA, we would have gone all the way," Trapp told the *Press-Telegram*. "They're the best team we played, and I think that we could be Kansas now."

BASKETBALL IN LONG BEACH

UCLA's Henry Bibby loses the ball while under pressure from four Long Beach players. Long Beach Press-Telegram *photo archive*.

"We were so close," wrote Tarkanian in his book, *Runnin' Rebel*. "That was probably the greatest game in Long Beach State history because UCLA was so historic."

Trapp would graduate after that bitter loss, going out with All-American honors and another conference player of the year award. The Detroit native

BASKETBALL IN LONG BEACH

became the first 49er to be drafted by the NBA, chosen as the fifth overall pick by the Atlanta Hawks. He would end his career with the Detroit Pistons after eight years.

Like Taylor, Trapp's life would also come to a tragic end; he died at the age of fifty-three in 2002 after complications from a stabbing in an argument with his roommate.

While beating UCLA in that '71 game certainty would have raised Long Beach State's national profile, nearly taking down the kings of college basketball was enough to put the school on the map.

What Could Have Been

Long Beach was a consensus Top 10 entering the 1971–72 season. *Inside Basketball* proclaimed that "it may be the best basketball school in the country" in due time.

Jerry Tarkanian during the 1973 season, his last at Long Beach State. *Long Beach Press-Telegram photo archive.*

BASKETBALL IN LONG BEACH

Tarkanian's fourth year kept the winning rolling, claiming an unprecedented third-straight PCAA title with another 10-0 league record and a fifty-four-game home winning streak.

The winning streak was thanks to one of the most notorious home court advantages in the nation at the Gold Mine, a 1,900-seat multipurpose gym that was erected in the 1950s. During the Tarkanian heyday, students and fans would pack the venue hours before tip-off to guarantee a spot. The benches were directly in front the crowds, and the gym routinely became swelteringly hot.

A few times, students brought wooden blocks to smash together to throw off opponents.

Powered by the junior Ratleff and Terry, the 49ers welcomed a bruising post player transfer in Leonard Gray from Kansas, who became eligible during the second semester.

Once again back in the tournament, the 49ers needed a "miracle," as Tarkanian, who had a famous habit of chewing a towel during tense moments, described it to the *Press-Telegram*. They survived Brigham Young 95–90 in overtime before thirteen thousand fans in Pocatello, Idaho. Ratleff led with twenty-one points, but it was sixteen huge points, including the go-ahead score from Lamont King, that sent the 49ers to the second round.

By comparison, Long Beach had a much easier time dispatching San Francisco by twenty points with sixteen points from both Ratleff and Terry.

And for the third-straight time—the second-straight time in the Western Regional Finals—Long Beach would face UCLA. The Bruins had graduated stars Rowe and Wicks from the previous season but still had point guard Henry Bibby and a pretty good sophomore center named Bill Walton, the eventual Naismith Player of the Year.

Tarkanian, as he outlined in his book, had the idea of constantly complimenting the Bruins and playing his team up as an overwhelming underdog leading up to the game in an effort to surprise UCLA. The players were also supposed to follow this script and did; that is, until center Nate Stephens went and blew it all up, calling Walton overrated.

Walton responded by dominating Stephens for nineteen points and eleven rebounds while Stephens scored just two points in the 73–57 loss.

That 1972 squad ranks high on the "what if?" spectrum of Long Beach State basketball thanks to the one who got away: George Gervin.

Gervin, nicknamed "the Iceman," was named one of the NBA's fifty greatest players, an ABA Rookie of the Year and an inductee in the Naismith Memorial Basketball Hall of Fame. But back in 1971, Gervin was an under-recruited player from Detroit with whom Tarkanian fell in love after seeing him play in person. Tarkanian got a tip from George Trapp's father and quickly locked up the Motor City boy to come out west.

"We came in as freshmen together. I didn't know he was a freshman," says McDonald. "When I came, he was already on the court playing pickup with Ratleff and all them…He was dunking on people. Putting on a show. I asked what year he was, and they said freshman. I said, 'You kidding me? You brought him in here with me? No way this guy isn't going to play.'"

But Gervin never did play, plagued by homesickness, fielding constant calls from his girlfriend. Trapp, a fellow Detroit native, was in charge of Gervin, but one day Trapp and Tarkanian were needed for a luncheon, so Trapp's duties fell to reserve Eric McWilliams.

The message from Tarkanian was clear: take care of George. Do whatever he wants.

What Gervin wanted was a ride to the airport.

"We never knew he was going home for good," says McDonald, a good friend of Gervin, who asked him to ride with him to the airport. "We thought he was going up for the weekend."

"If Tark had a gun, he would have shot both of them," says Ratleff with a laugh.

Gervin enrolled at Eastern Michigan University, averaging 29.5 points per game as a sophomore, but his college career was cut short after an infamous punch during a championship game that led to his withdrawal from school. He joined the ABA on his way to NBA fame with the San Antonio Spurs.

"God only knows how good they would have been," says longtime *Press-Telegram* writer and acclaimed basketball scribe Frank Burlison of the 1972 squad.

But Gervin was just one of the many talented players whom Tarkanian nearly lured to Long Beach. Tarkanian's recruiting prowess was no secret, and that's what made bigger programs view him as a threat and drew the attention of the NCAA.

Tarkanian nearly had future Lakers legend and Naismith Hall of Fame member Spencer Haywood playing for his very first team at Long Beach. Tarkanian served as the head coach of a junior college all-star team in the spring of 1968. Haywood, then a star at Trinidad State Junior College up in Colorado, made the team.

"When I played for Tark at the trials, I fell in love with him," Haywood told the *Las Vegas Review-Journal* in a 2013 article. "He was such a players' coach. He gave you that fire inside to play hard. He wanted me to come

BASKETBALL IN LONG BEACH

Jerry Tarkanian during the 1973 season. *Long Beach Press-Telegram photo archive.*

with him to Long Beach, and I actually took a visit there. Let me tell you, with the warm weather, the palm trees and the ocean, I was ready. But I had family back in Detroit; that's where I played my high school ball—at Pershing—so I felt obligated to go back home and play at UD."

Haywood did end up back in Detroit after leading the U.S. Olympic team to the 1968 gold medal, averaging 32.1 points per game. He became the nation's leading rebounder at 21.5 rebounds per game before heading to the ABA in 1969.

BASKETBALL IN LONG BEACH

But no loss was bigger in Tarkanian's mind than that of Los Angeles legend Raymond Lewis.

Tarkanian dedicated eight pages of his bio to the saga of recruiting Lewis, whom he called the "greatest player he ever saw."

Raised in Watts, Lewis stood just six-foot-one, combining agility that seemed "supernatural," as described by *Sports Illustrated*, and a jumper that was automatic. Lewis led tiny Verbum Dei High to three straight California Interscholastic Federation (CIF) championships.

Terry remembers Tarkanian and a crew of Long Beach players going to watch Lewis at a local Compton gym. Lewis played one-on-one with Long Beach State's Ray Gritton. By Terry's memory, it wasn't even close.

"Lewis was tearing up Ray. He was just going around him like nothing," said Terry. "He handled the ball like it was a yo-yo."

Lewis, at the time, was still a freshman in high school.

His play was quickly drawing the attention of programs all over the country, including UCLA, so much so that Wooden actually attended his games.

But Tarkanian had the inside track. Lewis trusted the coach enough to introduce Tarkanian to his mother, Ella Mae.

"[Lewis's] heart belonged to Jerry Tarkanian, then the coach at Long Beach State, which Tarkanian had turned into a national power. Tarkanian had been in contact with Lewis since the 10th grade, and during one stretch Tarkanian spent so much time with Lewis' mother that one day when the coach's wife Lois phoned him he called her Ella throughout the conversation," wrote Barry McDermott in a 1978 profile of Lewis in *Sports Illustrated*.

Soon enough, Lewis committed to Long Beach State and moved into the dorms. Tarkanian was satisfied with his biggest recruiting score in Long Beach State history; that is, until Tarkanian saw a news report that Lewis was enrolled at LA State. As the story goes, it all made sense when Lewis was seen driving around Watts in a brand-new Corvette. According to Tarkanian, he called LA State's head coach, Bob Miller, a good friend of his, and learned that Miller had indeed bought Lewis a car. Lewis had enrolled for summer classes. Long Beach didn't enroll until the fall, meaning Lewis was locked in at LA State for the year.

Lewis was everything he was advertised to be, scoring 73 points in a freshmen game against UC Santa Barbara and routing the UCLA freshmen by 15 points behind his 40 points. He averaged 38.9 points per game—the top mark for a freshman that season.

When he could finally play on varsity the following season, Lewis orchestrated a 107–104 double overtime win over number three Long Beach

BASKETBALL IN LONG BEACH

in 1973, scoring fifty-three points and setting the conference record. The game was so tense that Lewis's mother fainted and was taken by ambulance to the hospital in the final seconds.

"I knew you were going to do this to us," Tarkanian told Lewis after the game, as described in the *Press-Telegram*.

Lewis would bolt for the pros after that one varsity season, and his career spiraled downward from there. The Philadelphia 76ers drafted the star at the end of the first round, and Lewis was impressive in camp, outplaying the organization's top pick, Doug Collins, an Olympic star.

But Lewis would never play an official game with the 76ers. Contract negotiations went sour, and Lewis walked away and flew back home.

Lewis tried for several years to make it back to the NBA and several other professional basketball organizations, but he never caught on again. He passed away in 2001 due to complications following the amputation of his leg.

Tarkanian would spend just one more season at Long Beach, leading the team once again to a PCAA title and an NCAA berth. After defeating Weber State 88–75, the 49ers were upset by San Francisco, 77–67. Ratleff, who was coming off an Olympics appearance with the 1972 team that lost a highly controversial gold medal match against the Soviet Union, scored twelve points in his final game.

The 49ers did go out with one last bang, defeating legendary coach Al McGuire's Marquette team 76–66 in a sold-out Long Beach Arena to push the 49ers home winning streak to sixty-five games—the longest in the nation. It would eventually reach seventy-five.

The game featured seven technicals as Long Beach pulled away late before the record crowd of 12,987. It was the last home game for Tarkanian and the golden age of Long Beach State basketball.

After the '73 season, the NCAA, egged on by UCLA, really began putting the pressure on Tarkanian.

"As soon as he was successful, UCLA looked at him as a threat. J.D. Morgan, the athletic director at UCLA, particularly did not like threats," says McCormack. "He liked his kingdom just the way it was."

At the time, UNLV was pursuing the services of the coach, but Tarkanian decided to stay in Long Beach—until president Stephen Horn put an end to that.

"He had wanted to stay. Las Vegas had been wooing him…I said, 'Jerry, you're not staying here. The violations that we have found show clearly that you violated the NCAA rules and I'm not going to have a member of the coaching staff that does that.'" Horn's words were recounted in a

BASKETBALL IN LONG BEACH

Long Beach State preparing for a game at the Long Beach Arena, the final one of the 1973 season. This was the first sellout of the Long Beach Arena. *Long Beach Press-Telegram photo archive.*

2015 *Press-Telegram* article. "And he looked at me with those innocent eyes. I'll never forget this, he said, 'Dr. Horn, I haven't violated any NCAA rules.' He even blinked his eyes innocently. I said, 'No way.'"

Tarkanian, who passed away in 2015, went on to build UNLV to a national powerhouse and beat the NCAA's accusations in 1998, settling for millions. On his way to the Naismith Memorial Basketball Hall of Fame, Tarkanian won a national title, went to four Final Fours, racked up more than seven hundred wins and took the little college by the beach on one wild ride.

Lute Olson and the Greatest Team

Long Beach did not have to go far to find Tarkanian's replacement, reaching out to Long Beach City College's state championship–winning coach Lute Olson. Like Tarkanian, Olson had immediate success at the junior college level, his first college job after several seasons coaching at local high schools. Olson took the Vikings to the state title game in 1970, winning it all in 1971 and nearly twice more, finishing with a 103-22 career record.

Athletic director Dr. Lew Comer, who took over for Miller in 1971, called Olson the day after Tarkanian left and offered him the job during their first meeting.

"It was difficult because I really liked my job at City," says Olson. "But when Long Beach State contacted me, I said I would need some time because I knew the NCAA had spent a lot of time in the area checking on the program. I didn't want to leave a job like City [if probation was coming]."

LBCC and LBSU head coach Lute Olson. Long Beach Press-Telegram *photo archive*.

Comer assured Olson that no probation would be dealt to the program, but Olson was still torn between his success at City College and the highly sought-after job that Tarkanian had helped build. After going back and forth on the decision, Olson accepted the job, with a little advice from Kansas State's legendary coach Tex Winter.

Olson did lose Ratleff, who was drafted by the Houston Rockets with the number six pick, but the team Olson was left with still might have been the best team in program history.

Olson inherited the bruising Gray, point guard Rick Aberagg, Glenn McDonald and star Roscoe Pondexter. He also inherited Roscoe's younger brother Clifton, a Tarkanian recruit and a prep All-American at San Joaquin Memorial High School, where he averaged twenty-five points per game and sixteen rebounds.

Olson went as far as to call the six-foot-eight Clifton the best freshman prospect he had ever seen outside of Kareem Abdul-Jabbar when he was at UCLA, earning him the title of the best big man prospect ever brought to Long Beach.

BASKETBALL IN LONG BEACH

The team also featured a pair of stud transfers in six-foot-eight Carlos Mina, who led the Mexican national team in scoring and played freshman ball at USC before transferring to Imperial Valley Junior College, and six-foot-six Bob Gross from the University of Seattle. Gross averaged twenty-three points per game on the freshman squad before leaving for Harbor Junior College.

"They were so good it was incredible," says Gary Anderson, a former player for Olson and longtime coach at Long Beach City College who attended practices. "It wasn't even fair."

But as a new coach, one with a much stricter coaching approach than Tarkanian and inheriting players he did not recruit, Olson and the team bumped heads early on.

"At times, he would make sure you knew he was the head coach," says Glenn McDonald, who served as a mediator between Olson and team. "Because he had guys that didn't really want to play for him because he was new. 'I came here to play for Tark'—that kind of stuff.

"But as time went on, they came to respect him," says McDonald. "They saw that he knew the game."

The 49ers spilt their first two games, a two-point loss to Colorado, whose players were sucking down oxygen on the bench while Long Beach dealt with the thin air, before ripping off nine straight wins.

After the 10-1 start, Olson and the team were dealt the news that the program would be put on probation and banned from the postseason for three years. The phone call came during an early January practice in preparation for a tough road trip.

The NCAA called the twenty-six violations, which also included the football program, "among the most serious" it had ever encountered.

McDonald and Roscoe Pondexter were also ruled ineligible after allegations that they'd had tests taken for them, but they were cleared after a hearing conducted by the school.

Olson came to find out through his wife, Bobbi, who was friends with Comer's wife and other wives in the administration, that the school knew sanctions were coming down and had misled its new hire.

"Well, they weren't truthful," says Olson. "If they had said we may be going on probation, it might have been different.

"I would have been happy in Long Beach," says Olson. "I really loved my time at City College, and if the sanctions hadn't come down or they would have told the truth about them, I would have stayed around."

Despite the drama, Long Beach refused to collapse, going on to finish 24-2—12-0 in the PCAA—still the best winning percentage in school history.

BASKETBALL IN LONG BEACH

Roscoe Pondexter going for a loose ball as his brother, Clifton, looks on. Long Beach Press-Telegram *photo archive*.

"They recovered so well. We were so far superior to anyone in the conference," says Olson. "Credit to the players; they were like, OK, this is the way it is, let's prove we are a team that could have been successful."

Olson was asked to sign an extension, but that wasn't going to happen after the deceit.

"I wasn't going to work for someone I couldn't take their word for," says Olson.

Schools were interested in Olson's services after he weathered the storm that season. Olson eventually accepted the head-coaching job at the University of Iowa. Back in the Midwest, he led the Hawkeyes to five NCAA berths, including a Final Four trip in 1980. From Iowa, Olson built Arizona into a national power, winning a national title in 1997 on his way to the Naismith Memorial Basketball Hall of Fame.

Long Beach was left to wonder what that 1974 team could have done in March.

"When we walked into an arena, we knew we were going to win. I don't know what we would have done in the NCAA Tournament…would we have given UCLA another run?" asks McDonald. "They had a really great team with Walton and Keith Wilkes, but I just honestly feel we could have beat that team."

"[Olson] told me that the team he inherited from Tarkanian might be the most talented team he has ever coached," says Anderson.

"Yeah, I think so. At Arizona with Steve Kerr in 1988 was great, and certainly the NCAA championship team is there, but that team at Long Beach State…it would have been interesting to see what could have happened," says Olson. "That team would have had a shot to win the whole thing."

Tex Winter

Long Beach State decided to turn to the bench to fill the head-coaching position vacated by Olson, hiring assistant Dwight Jones. Jones, who played collegiately at Pepperdine, also served as an assistant under Tarkanian.

Jones inherited a team that lost all five starters. Gray, McDonald and the Pondexter brothers earned All-American status before heading to the NBA. Gray was selected by the Seattle Supersonics and McDonald by the Boston Celtics (winning a championship in 1976). Roscoe was also taken by the Celtics, while his younger brother Clifton was selected by the Chicago Bulls.

Jones did return Gross and Mina, with Gross going on to win the PCAA Player of the Year award, the sixth-straight POY award for Long Beach, and All-American status. Jones and the 49ers finished first in the PCAA with an 8-2 conference record, but probation kept them out of the postseason.

Long Beach finished first again the next year, the last year of probation. It wasn't until 1976–77 that the 49ers headed back to the NCAA Tournament, finishing in first place for the eighth consecutive time.

The return to the postseason was powered by one of the best recruiting classes the 49ers ever put together, headlined by three prep All-Americans, most notably Michael Wiley, the six-foot-eight Long Beach Poly star. Lloyd McMillian, a standout transfer from Loyola-Marymount, also became eligible.

BASKETBALL IN LONG BEACH

Donnie Martin, Francois Wise, Michael Wiley and James Hughes. *Long Beach State photo archive.*

Long Beach clinched the PCAA crown in the new conference tournament format, defeating Cal State Fullerton in overtime and San Jose State.

The 49ers headed back to Pocatello, Idaho, for a first-round meeting with Idaho State before ten thousand fans. Despite thirty-four combined points from McMillian and Wiley, Idaho State came out on top, 83–72, dominating the 49ers in the paint.

BASKETBALL IN LONG BEACH

Jones coached one more season at Long Beach and finished fifth in the conference. He resigned from his position and became principal of Rivera Middle School in Pico Rivera. Jones had an aggressive approach with the team that spilled over to dealings with the administration, and this might have aided his departure.

"Dwight was a really good coach. Kept them competitive during the probation," said McCormack. "If Dwight could have stayed and managed his relationships with the administration, [Long Beach] might have been one of those mid-level programs to kind of sustain it."

Jones still ranks third in school history with a winning percentage of .636 (70-40), behind Olson and Tarkanian.

Feeling the need the get a home-run hire, the administration made a play for and landed Tex Winter. It was Winter who had encouraged Olson to take the Long Beach State job, and now it was his.

Winter, a former player at Compton Junior College, was lured away from Northwestern University but made his name at Kansas State. After becoming the youngest head coach in the nation at Marquette at age twenty-eight, Winter spent fifteen years at Kansas State, where he led the Wildcats to eight conference titles, four Elite Eights and two trips to the Final Four. At the time of his hiring, Winter ranked ninth in active career wins, with 376, marking the third eventual Naismith Hall of Fame coach to call Long Beach home.

But unlike his predecessors Tarkanian and Olson, Winter never had the success those two coaches produced.

After a fourth-place finish in his inaugural season, Winter and the 49ers finished second in the conference with an 11-3 mark, pulling off wins against Wichita State, Oklahoma State, Colorado and Marquette.

After picking up an eight-point win over UC Irvine in the first round of the PCAA Tournament, the 49ers survived Pacific 72–70, behind Wiley's jumper with fifteen seconds left, for a spot in the championship game.

But the 49ers fell to number four seed San Jose State 57–55, missing a shot as time expired. Winter and the team did receive an invite to the National Invitational Tournament, losing in the second round to Tarkanian and UNLV, 90–81.

The next few years were never as good for Winter, with third-, fourth- and seventh-place finishes in his final seasons.

It's a puzzling five years of mediocrity under a coach who is highly regarded as one of the most brilliant basketball minds of all time thanks to his development of the modern triangle or triple-post offense. After leaving Long Beach in 1983, and telling the media he was retiring from coaching,

BASKETBALL IN LONG BEACH

Tex Winter drawing up a play on the hardwood on December 24, 1978. Long Beach Press-Telegram *photo archive*.

Winter joined the Chicago Bulls as an assistant in 1985, teaching his offense to a young superstar, Michael Jordan. Legendary head coach Phil Jackson was hired by the Bulls in 1989. Winter and Jackson went on to win ten championships together with the Bulls and Lakers.

"We would go scouting, and it was amazing how he could diagram the other team's plays," says Ratleff, an assistant under Winter. "I'm trying to draw up the first cut of the first play, he's already got the whole play and already starting the next one!"

Observers of the Winter era point to a lack of the right players to carry out his offense as the main reason the 49ers did not enjoy greater success.

"I think for the most part, it was recruiting wasn't something he really enjoyed. For Tex's stuff to work, you have to buy into it, you have to be a disciplined player," says McCormack. "I think maybe the players had a little trouble understanding him, and maybe he felt he wasn't as successful communicating to them."

Winter had several standout players during his tenure in Wiley, Michael Zeno, Craig Dykema, Craig Hodges, Rickey Williams and Francois Wise but never a dominant force like Ratleff or Trapp.

That doesn't stop people from remembering the Winter years as some of the best in Long Beach history.

"Those were some of the most enjoyable years of my life," says McCormack. "The guy was an absolute genius. He was a genius as a coach and a genius as a human being. He was as likable and accessible as any man I have ever met."

The Decline and Rise: Joe Harrington and Seth Greenberg

From the moment Tarkanian left Long Beach, the program fell under the "Curse of Tarkanian," as McCormack describes it. The administration was constantly trying to recapture the immediate success that "Tark the Shark" had been able to accomplish.

After the Tex Winter experiment provided underwhelming results, Long Beach pulled Dave Buss from Tarkanian's bench at UNLV. Buss had gone to Las Vegas from the University of Wisconsin–Green Bay, which he had built into a Division II power. Buss, hired by Vince Lombardi, had built the Green Bay program from scratch in 1969, taking the team to two national title games and finishing with a 271-102 record.

The result of his move to Long Beach was the worst season in Long Beach State history since 1966. The 49ers won just nine games, and Buss was promptly fired.

Like its counterparts at Long Beach City College, which had hired Charlie Church in the 1950s, Long Beach hired high school coaching

BASKETBALL IN LONG BEACH

legend Ron Palmer from Long Beach Poly in 1984. Palmer, who would end up coaching for twenty-five years at Poly, counting 601 wins, was coming off a magical 1984 season in which the Jackrabbits went 31-2, winning the state and mythical national title. Palmer was hired in April, with just ten days to recruit, but he still managed to sign eight freshmen, including Morlon Wiley, Palmer's star at Poly and the younger brother of Michael Wiley.

But the jump to Division I didn't work out; the 49ers won just eleven games in Palmer's first two seasons against forty-five losses. Palmer won twelve games his third year but then resigned, citing stress that had led to weight loss and sickness.

"I've got to get away from the pressure, and the biggest pressure comes from me," Palmer told the *Los Angeles Times*. "No one here has said, 'You have to win.'"

The next hire would be one that would mark the steady rise of the program. Athletic director John Kasser's national search landed the 49ers' Joe Harrington all the way from the East Coast. Harrington played collegiately at the University of Maryland under Bud Millikan and returned to serve as an assistant under National Collegiate Basketball Hall of Fame member Lefty Driesell for a decade.

After landing his second head-coaching job at George Mason, which he led to the Division I level for seven years, Harrington headed out west to try to end the curse.

Harrington stayed just three seasons in Southern California and finished with a 53-36 record, but he built a foundation that would sustain the 49ers for nearly a decade.

Harrington brought with him a top-notch coaching staff with assistant Dereck Whittenburg, who won a national title at NC State as a player under Jim Valvano and played under legendary high school coach Morgan Wooten at DeMatha Catholic High School in Maryland, and associate head coach Seth Greenberg.

Greenberg was one of the top assistants in the nation, with stops on his resume at Columbia, Miami, Pittsburgh and the University of Virginia when it reached the Final Four. It was a matter of when, not if, when it came to Greenberg and a head-coaching position.

In Harrington's first year, the 49ers finished fourth in the conference, which became known as the Big West in 1988, the program's highest finish since 1982. Long Beach was bounced in the first round of the NIT, but it might as well have been the Elite Eight.

BASKETBALL IN LONG BEACH

Joe Harrington smiling during a game. Long Beach Press-Telegram *photo archive*.

"What Harrington and his staff did last year was nothing short of phenomenal," wrote the 49ers' media guide the following season. "To coin a phrase, 'The Pride is Back.'"

Harrington's third season was the breakout year; the coach was already talking about that season the year before at the Big West Tournament. The staff pulled a top twenty recruiting class that featured transfer Kevin Cutler and a six-foot-five All-American from Cleveland High School in Los Angeles, Lucious Harris.

"People knew he was good, but people didn't know how good he was," said Burlison. "Everyone thought he would go to Kansas."

BASKETBALL IN LONG BEACH

LBSU head coach Seth Greenberg pushing his team during the first-round NCAA game against Illinois, March 19, 1993. Long Beach Press-Telegram *photo archive.*

Behind Harris, who won Big West Freshman of the Year after leading the team in scoring (14.3 points per game), the 49ers finished 23-9, the best season since Lute Olson's one year.

Once again, Long Beach was back in the NIT, defeating Arizona State before falling to Hawaii in Honolulu.

Harrington was gone after that, wooed by the thought of coaching in the Big Eight at the University of Colorado, a school he said reminded him of his alma mater, the University of Maryland.

But unlike in the past, when a search was needed, the Athletic Department had the easy task of hiring Greenberg as head coach.

Greenberg, one of the best recruiters in the nation, called the hiring a dream come true for him and went about continuing to build what his former boss had left behind.

Greenberg's first two teams finished in sixth and fourth place, respectively, with the program's third NIT trip in five seasons.

Like Harrington, Greenberg had his breakout season in year three, racking up a 22-10 record and the biggest win in school history.

On January 25, Long Beach State headed into one of the most iconic college basketball arenas in the sport's history: the University of Kansas's Allen Field House.

BASKETBALL IN LONG BEACH

The Jayhawks, 17-1 and the number one team in the country, entered as a seventeen-point favorite over a 49ers team that had lost by thirty-four points to VCU two days earlier.

But the 49ers shocked Kansas and the college basketball world with a 64–49 win, shooting 62.8 percent in the upset. Harris, who had turned down the Jayhawks to play for Long Beach, scored twenty-four points, breaking the school scoring record in the process.

"Long Beach was so good, and the crowd was just silent," says Burlison, then the beat writer. "One of the most remarkable things. Everything just went well for them."

It would be hard to choose another highlight of that season after that win, but the 49ers did go on to win the Big West Tournament as the number four seed with a 70–62 win over New Mexico State.

Making their first NCAA Tournament appearance since 1977, the 49ers took on the number six seed Illinois. Long Beach grabbed a one-point lead with 1:38 left on a Harris layup (twenty-seven points), but two straight baskets from the Fighting Illini sealed the 75–72 win for Illinois.

That game ended the careers of two of the best and most interesting 49ers in the program's history in Harris and forward Bryon Russell. Harris was known as a shy and reserved individual who spent his time raising canaries and pigeons growing up, lending him the nickname "Birdman." Tending to his birds kept Harris away from the courts growing up, but when he did play, he dominated opponents. Harris is the only player in Long Beach State history to score more than 2,000 points in his career (2,312) and still sits as the Big West's career leader for points.

Harris was taken in the second round of the 1993 NBA draft by the Dallas Mavericks. He would jump to the 76ers in 1996 before finding a home with the New Jersey Nets for seven years, helping them to two NBA Finals appearances.

"You could make an argument that he was the best player in Long Beach history. He got them back to the tournament for the first time in sixteen years," said Burlison. "Probably the best senior season for anyone since the Tarkanian years."

Russell was a standout at San Bernardino High School, winning a CIF title in 1989. He would spend thirteen seasons in the NBA, nine with the Utah Jazz, the team that drafted him with the forty-fifth pick in the second round.

Russell reached two NBA Finals with the Jazz, becoming part of Finals history as the defender of Michael Jordan as he drained the '98

BASKETBALL IN LONG BEACH

Right: Lucious Harris would go on to become Long Beach State and the Big West Conference's all-time leading scorer, both of which records still stand today. *Long Beach State photo archive.*

Below: LBSU head coach Seth Greenberg, battling chickenpox, has to give team instructions from his office. Long Beach Press-Telegram *photo archive.*

51

BASKETBALL IN LONG BEACH

Finals game winner in Game 6 (although many say Jordan pushed off Russell for the shot).

"I always say, he had to cheat me to beat me," Russell told the *Daily Bulletin*. "I'm a Michael fan, too, but they weren't going to call a foul on that play."

Both Russell and Harris joined Ratleff as the only three former Long Beach players to have their jerseys retired.

Greenberg had a special player in the wings to replace the star power of Russell and Harris in James Cotton, a highly touted scorer from St. John Bosco. Cotton was slated to redshirt his freshman season (1993–94), but Greenberg decided to activate the freshman in the second game of the season.

Cotton went on to average 11.4 points per game and win Big West Freshman of the Year honors. Greenberg called his decision to activate Cotton the "best decision of my coaching career."

Things seemed to only get better under Greenberg. The next year, Long Beach State opened the Walter Pyramid, a $22 million structure with a capacity of five thousand, to replace the legendary Gold Mine Gym.

The Pyramid opened before 5,021 fans in an ESPN-televised game on November 30, 1994, as the 49ers defeated the University of Detroit Mercy, 71–64. Greenberg would once again lead Long Beach back to the NCAA Tournament after the program's second Big West Tournament championship in three seasons, defeating UNLV in overtime. But the 49ers were without Cotton for the entire year after the sophomore suffered a severely sprained ankle before the season started.

Long Beach headed to Boise, Idaho, to play the number four seed Utah in the first round. The 49ers struggled shooting the ball, hitting just 14.3 percent from the three-point line and 46.2 percent from the free throw line. Utah used its noticeable size advantage to out rebound the Big West champs in a 76–64 win.

By now, the bigger programs had taken notice of the success Greenberg was having at Long Beach. UNLV and USC began requesting to interview the head coach, leading to an upgraded contract with the 49ers.

The next year, Greenberg's sixth, the 49ers finished first in the Big West—for the first time since 1977. But Long Beach was upset by Utah State in its first round of the conference tournament, finishing the season at 17-11. Nonetheless, Greenberg established himself as the most successful coach in Long Beach State history after Tarkanian.

But in April, Greenberg was gone, having accepted the head-coaching job at the University of South Florida. There are many in the Long Beach community who felt Greenberg always had one foot out the door while leading the 49ers, constantly searching for the next jump.

"He was ambitious and young; he wanted to climb up the ladder. He was Harrington's right-hand man," says Burlison. "He certainly left the program in much better shape than when he got there."

Greenberg told the *Press-Telegram* that this wasn't the case, but he felt that South Florida's conference, Conference USA, offered a bigger national stage and opportunity.

"I feel certain that a team from the Conference USA will win a national championship more than just one time," Greenberg told the *Press-Telegram*. "I base this on long term…that this program can get me where I want to go."

Once again, Long Beach State was a steppingstone.

Dan Monson

On paper, Greenberg's successor, Wayne Morgan, was a home run. Morgan spent twelve years as an assistant to one of best in the business: Syracuse's Jim Boeheim. What made him all the more appealing was that Morgan was Boeheim's lead recruiter.

But on paper and on the court are two very different things. After failing to record a winning season and with just one win in the conference tournament in his first three seasons, Morgan was already feeling the pressure from the administration.

Morgan was able to buy more time with a 24-6 record the following season—15-1 in the Big West behind the conference's Player of the Year in Mate Milisa—but for the second-straight season, the 49ers could not get past the tournament semifinals.

The former Syracuse assistant would last two more seasons, resigning with two years still left on his contract.

Larry Reynolds would become the fifteenth head coach in Long Beach State history, hired off his reputation in five seasons at Cal State San Bernardino, where he built the program from nothing to a Division II power, leading the team to two Elite Eight appearances and an overall 110-35 record. Reynolds also served as an assistant at the University of San Francisco and UC Riverside.

Like Buss and Palmer before him, the jump to the Division I level didn't pan out for Reynolds, as Long Beach won just eleven games in his first two seasons, failing to qualify for the tournament. But with the infusion of junior

BASKETBALL IN LONG BEACH

college talent like Aaron Nixon, Jibril Hodges, Kejuan Johnson and Travis Reed, the 49ers began to win.

In Reynolds's fourth season, Long Beach went 18-12 with a high-scoring offense (83.3 points per game) that led the nation as the 49ers advanced to the Big West championship game behind Nixon and Johnson. Nixon drilled a buzzer-beating three-pointer in the Big West semifinals for a 75–73 win over UC Irvine before the 49ers fell 78–70 to Pacific.

Yet looking over the record books will show the 2005–06 season as a 4-12 endeavor, with an eighth-place finish in the conference.

Long Beach would forfeit fourteen wins two years later, after an NCAA investigation revealed improper benefits, improper transportation, phone contacts and "unethical conduct" by members of the coaching staff.

Those issues arose with the 2005–06 recruiting class, which featured six junior college transfers who were not eligible for admission. According to the report, the program was involved in the registration and payment of community college classes for three of the junior college transfers during the fall of 2004 and the summer of 2005.

In addition to NCAA sanctions, the school would self-impose sanctions that added up to three years' probation, loss of scholarships for two years and no recruiting of junior college players during the probation.

Knowledge of the investigation came forth during Reynolds's final season in Long Beach (2006–07), the best season for the program since 1995, with a 24-8 record, a Big West title, a conference player of the year in Nixon and an NCAA berth.

Long Beach headed to Columbus, Ohio, to face the number five seed Tennessee but was blown out 121–86 to end the season. Reynolds's contract was not renewed.

Early on in that final season for Reynolds, the eventual successor, Dan Monson, was in the process of resigning from the University of Minnesota seven games into the season.

Two days after Long Beach State suffered a thirty-point loss to UCLA, all the way in Minnesota, Monson held a press conference to announce his resignation after seven years at the helm.

It was a low moment for a coach who was not that far removed from helping create a dynasty.

Monson was the son of well-regarded college coach Don Monson, who spent fourteen years as the head coach at Idaho and the University of Oregon. The elder Monson led the Vandals to the Sweet Sixteen in 1982, still the best season in school history.

BASKETBALL IN LONG BEACH

The younger Monson decided to go into coaching while attending Idaho while his father was leading the program. Monson got his first college gig as an assistant at UAB after several seasons as head coach of Oregon City High School.

After UAB, Monson was hired as an assistant at Gonzaga in 1988 under Dan Fitzgerald, eventually taking over for Fitzgerald in 1997. Monson would lead the Bulldogs for just two seasons, but they would be the two seasons that helped turn the program into a national power.

Gonzaga went 24-10 in Monson's first season and 28-7 in year two as the Bulldogs advanced to the Elite Eight, knocking off number seven Minnesota, number two Stanford and number six Florida as the number ten seed before falling to eventual national champion Connecticut 67–62.

The Elite Eight run officially made Monson one of the hottest coaches in the country. The second-year head coach accepted the position at Minnesota even though the program was on the verge of being handed down NCAA sanctions for academic fraud.

With the Golden Gophers, Monson took the program to four NIT appearances and an NCAA Tournament berth in 2005 but never finished higher than fourth in the Big Ten.

Since Monson's departure in 1999, Gonzaga, under Mark Few, has reached sixteen straight NCAA Tournaments and is now a national power.

Now, in 2006, the man who helped build Gonzaga was on the verge of walking away from coaching.

"I didn't know if I ever wanted to coach again," says Monson. "I was stung and burned out. I had three or four months to reflect."

Monson was in talks with San Diego and the University of Denver despite the burnout but never applied to Long Beach, and that was one of the school's first questions when it called him.

"I don't feel like it fit me," said Monson. "The reputation of Long Beach has been a lot of junior college players."

However, after the Reynolds fiasco with transfers, the Athletic Department was bent on changing that formula and saw Monson as the man to foster that new chapter.

With Long Beach and Monson on the same page, the 49ers hired their new head coach in April, and it became clear to a reenergized Monson that the job would not be easy.

Monson describes that first season as "painful"—the team finished 6-25, with just seven scholarship players, three of whom Monson would end up dismissing.

BASKETBALL IN LONG BEACH

But the sixteen-hour days Monson and the staff were putting in soon paid off. The 49ers were soon in the hunt for the Big West, finishing second and third in the regular season the next two season and falling to UC Santa Barbara by five in the 2010 Big West championship game.

Monson's program was built on the foundation of one of Long Beach State's greatest recruiting classes in school history, known as the "Fab Four": T.J. Robinson from Connecticut, Eugene Phelps of LA, Long Beach Jordan's Larry Anderson and point guard Casper Ware of Gahr High School in nearby Cerritos.

Anderson would go on to win the Big West Freshman of the Year Award in 2009 and the Defensive Player of the Year Award in 2012, and Robinson is still the career rebounding leader at Long Beach, with 1,208, and number five in scoring.

But Ware was the headliner. The son of Casper Ware Sr., a local street ball legend, the undersized but scrappy guard won back-to-back Big West Player of the Year Awards in 2011 and 2012, joining George Trapp and Ed Ratleff as the only two-time winners.

After making the Big West Tournament championship game in 2010, the Fab Four led the program to a regular-season conference championship the following year but once again fell to the Gauchos in the title game, setting up just one last chance to make the NCAA Tournament.

"That year felt like a lot of pressure," says Monson. "I didn't want that to be the best group of players to never go to the tournament."

Behind those four starting seniors, Long Beach caught the attention of the college basketball world in upsetting number nine Pittsburgh 86–76 on the road behind a career-high twenty-eight points from Ware. It was the first victory over a top ten team for Long Beach since its upset of number one Kansas in 1993.

Long Beach also had narrow losses to powerhouses Kansas, Louisville and North Carolina—all within single digits and all on the road.

The 49ers cruised toward their second-straight regular-season crown, but disaster struck in the finale against Cal State Fullerton as Anderson injured his knee, and the remainder of his season looked bleak. Long Beach ended up losing by three points, ruining a perfect conference record.

"I went home and broke down emotionally," says Monson. "I couldn't stand the thought of [Larry] not getting that opportunity to play in the NCAA Tournament."

By the time the Big West Tournament came around, Monson was also dealing with the sudden illness of his father, Don, seventy-eight at the time and rushed to the hospital, where they diagnosed an infection in his leg.

Despite the loss of Anderson and Monson's time spent at the hospital tending to his father, Long Beach made it back to the Big West championship game, once again facing UC Santa Barbara.

Behind Ware, who put in thirty-three points, the Fab Four finally got their NCAA Tournament berth in a game that felt part destiny.

"I remember when Casper hit a three right in front of me with about four or five minutes left in the game and got fouled, and it went in," says Monson. "Picking him off the floor, I remember saying to him, 'You are not going to let us lose this game.' It wasn't bragging. It was a revelation that just came to me…like I said it to myself."

Long Beach headed to Oregon for its ninth appearance in the NCAAs, facing number five seed New Mexico State. The whole week leading up to the game, Monson was "obsessed" with Anderson's health.

Anderson did end up playing, but not at full strength, as Long Beach fell 75–68, a late two-point lead by the 49ers not enough.

Despite the graduation of the core seniors—Ware signed as a free agent with the Philadelphia 76ers—Long Beach still had a star in James Ennis, who led the 49ers to their third-straight regular-season crown and an NIT appearance. Ennis, a transfer from Ventura College, would win the Big West Player of the Year Award, the third-straight 49er to win the honor, as well as All-American status. The senior was drafted in the second round of the NBA draft and now stars with the Miami Heat.

The Fab Four set in place a new generation for Long Beach State, a new page in a still-growing history.

"That by far is the best recruiting class as a group. They were all good friends, but they all had jealousies toward each other," says Monson, who surpassed Tarkanian as the program's win leader in 2015. "The last year was so great because they finally realized they needed each other, while the first three years they spent a lot of time trying to prove that they didn't, that they could do things on their own. They took some beat downs…but that made them into a group that will always be remembered as a group instead of as individuals."

2
Long Beach State Women

The Long Beach State women's basketball team may not have gotten as much air time as the university's men's team over the years, but there's no doubt that the women's 49er history is at least as rich.

Founding the 49ers

In the fall of 1962, an assistant professor named Dr. Frances Schaafsma decided that the school should have a women's sports program. That was a fairly revolutionary idea given that this was still a full decade before Title IX would be passed, guaranteeing women equal opportunity in high school and college sports.

Schaafsma's first move was to start a basketball team, one that she would coach for the next seventeen years. She also founded the college's women's volleyball team in 1964, coaching both teams at the same time until 1970. She wrote books on fundamentals and drills for women's basketball and volleyball, some of the earliest-known volumes on the subject.

But it wasn't enough for Shaafsma to simply start a women's basketball program; she was also determined to see it done right and to see the team be successful. In the 49ers' first season, they went 4-0, in a series of games so informal that no official box scores were kept. No official university records exist for the program's inaugural season.

BASKETBALL IN LONG BEACH

Dr. Frances Shaafsma coaching in her final season with Long Beach State. Press-Telegram *file photo*.

BASKETBALL IN LONG BEACH

Part of the reason for the limited schedule was that there weren't many other college teams to play. That quickly changed over the next few years, as UCLA, USC, Cal State Fullerton and other Southern California teams began to field teams.

Schaafsma, a graduate of Long Beach State who went on to get her doctorate from USC, was wildly successful in coaching the 49ers on a shoestring budget. The team wouldn't have its first losing record until the 1992–93 campaign, three decades after she first posted paper around the campus, calling for players to come and try out.

Schaafsma coached the team for its first seventeen years, posting an overall record of 209-73. The team won the first-ever Southern California Collegiate women's basketball title in 1963, led by Lorie Lindahl, who was also a star on Schaafsma's volleyball team. Lindahl would play professionally for ten years after earning three All-American honors and then began her post-playing life at Jordan, where she coached the Panthers' high school team for several years.

Schaafsma guided the 49ers through the ever-evolving world of SoCal college basketball as her teams competed in four different conferences. The 49ers didn't lose a game until their fourth season, beating everyone in their second season by at least twenty points. Finally, after a 17-0 start over three years, they lost to Cal State Fullerton during their fourth campaign. The 49ers either went undefeated or won a conference title in each of their first fourteen seasons.

But while Schaafsma led the 49ers to title after title in such long-lost conferences as the ECCSCC and SCWIAC, it was her replacement who would steer the ship into the NCAA era for women's basketball and put Long Beach on the map for good.

JOAN BONVICINI

Joan Bonvicini was an assistant under Schaafsma, a young firebrand who was already known as a peerless recruiter just a few years into her career. When Schaafsma moved into administration, becoming Long Beach State's women's athletic director and helping guide the NCAA's policy as it began to organize women's sports, Bonvicini waited in the wings.

"Fran was a terrific mentor for me," says Bonvicini, now the coach at Seattle University. "The people who were the mentors and leaders during that era, they had to fight for every penny for the women's program."

BASKETBALL IN LONG BEACH

Joan Bonvicini elevated the program to new heights. Press-Telegram *file photo*.

After Schaafsma's retirement from coaching, Bonvicini was offered a job at West Point—it came with a large salary, a book contract and a house on the base. Meanwhile, Long Beach State took its time making its decision, even while West Point's athletic director was calling Bonvicini twice daily, at 6:00 a.m. and 6:00 p.m. Finally, Long Beach State athletic director Perry Moore pulled the trigger, and Bonvicini accepted. Her salary for 1979–80, her first season, was $24,000.

In the twelve seasons Bonvicini coached the team, the 49ers made the postseason every year as she racked up a 325-71 record. Since Bonvicini left for the University of Arizona after the 1990–91 season, the Beach has made it back to the NCAA Tournament only once.

An All-American basketball player herself at Southern Connecticut State, Bonvicini knew how to talk to elite talent. She started by recruiting the best player in school history right out of the gate, signing LaTaunya Pollard, a talented player out of East Chicago.

"I refused to get a no," Bonvicini says of her recruiting style. Pollard committed to the 49ers on a recruiting visit but later visited UNLV and changed her mind. Bonvicini's goal was to bring in a blue chip recruit every year, and she knew she had to land Pollard.

"I told our AD I have to go to Chicago right now—I begged him," Bonvicini says. "I told him, 'She's going to be the best you've ever seen,' and I told him if he didn't let me go, it would be his fault she didn't come. So I took a redeye flight. I drove straight to the high school from the airport and got there at 8:00 a.m., talked to LaTaunya, and she recommitted."

BASKETBALL IN LONG BEACH

Pollard set every school record possible, earning two-time All-American honors and setting career marks for points scored, field goals made and free throws made. She was also second in school history in rebounds, earning Wade Trophy honors in 1983, making her the school's first (and only) National Player of the Year.

"She scored over three thousand points without the three-point line," Bonvicini laughs. "Her first game, which was my first game as a head coach, she made her first ten shots—and none of them were layups. On the tenth one, I fell off the bleachers. It was unbelievable."

Pollard was named to the 1980 Olympic team, which boycotted the games, and is one of just three 49ers to have their numbers retired. After the 1981 season, the Beach finished number two in the nation in the AP poll, and Bonvicini earned Division I Coach of the Year honors. Pollard went on to an eight-year pro career in Europe, including one game that saw her score ninety-nine points in the Italian Championship League.

LaTaunya Pollard poses with the 1983 Wade Trophy, given to the best collegiate women's player in America. *Long Beach State media guide.*

After Pollard graduated (having averaged almost thirty points a game in her career), the team continued to bring in top talent and routinely finished seasons ranked in the top ten nationally. The crowds grew in the sweltering Gold Mine Gym on campus as Bonvicini's Fastbreak Boosters helped to pack in the fans for sellout after sellout. The Beach's brand of basketball was fast paced with pressing defenses; Bonvicini said she wanted to coach a style that would utilize her team's athleticism and be fun for fans to watch.

BASKETBALL IN LONG BEACH

FINALLY, FINAL FOUR

Although the 49ers were one of the top teams in the nation, the Final Four remained just out of Bonvicini's grasp. "To get to the Final Four, you have to have a lot of good things going for you," she says now.

The team finally got there in back-to-back years in March 1987 and 1988. In '87, the team got off to a 20-1 start, the best in program history. Having All-American Cindy Brown on the team certainly helped, and when Bonvicini added Penny Toler, whom she calls the best ball-handling guard she ever saw, things took off.

"Good guards will keep you in every game, but I felt in order to win championships, you need posts," says Bonvicini. "And we had them."

The Beach ran a transition offense, up-tempo with shots going early in the shot clock. The team's average points per game ballooned to over ninety, and it led the league in scoring. Bonvicini, who wouldn't call off the press until her team led by thirty, was accused of running up the score. "We never tried to, but we never told the kids not to play hard," she says. "It was a lot of fun, the style we played."

In 1987, the 49ers beat Washington, Mississippi and Ohio State to reach the Final Four, where they ran into Tennessee, the eventual national champion. The Beach actually went into the game favored and led Pat Summitt's Lady Vols by ten points at the half.

Cindy Brown goes up for the ball during one of her All-American seasons. Press-Telegram *file photo*.

64

BASKETBALL IN LONG BEACH

But the game became more physical in the second half, and Tennessee took the lead. "I don't care what they say, in the men's or women's game, the officials don't want to decide the game that late in the season," says Bonvicini. "It was called completely differently—I think as a coach, I could have made some adjustments better. It was a tough lesson."

Some of the hardware the 49ers collected under Shaafsma and Bonvicini. *Long Beach State media guide.*

BASKETBALL IN LONG BEACH

The 49ers would lose by ten to end their best season ever at 33-3, and the Vols would go on to win Summitt her first national championship a few days later. Long Beach State was left to lick its wounds and think about the next season.

Cindy Brown finished that year with the second-highest point total in NCAA history (974 points) and would go on to win a gold medal at the 1988 Olympics. Just three years after she graduated, she was playing professionally in Japan when she was rear-ended by a drunk driver, a serious accident that smashed her head into the windshield, causing nerve damage and all but ending what was at that time one of the brightest careers in American women's hoops.

The Beach missed the presence of future LBSU Hall of Famers Brown and Margaret Mohr but plunged ahead in 1987–88 with Toler and Dana Wilkerson, the best guard combo in the nation. The team went 28-6 and ran through Colorado, Washington and Iowa in a regional hosted in the Gold Mine, making its second straight Final Four appearance.

But again, the Beach fell a little short in the Final Four, dropping a tough game to Auburn, 68–55. "They played a matchup zone, and we didn't do a good job breaking it down," says Bonvicini.

The next year, the Beach returned its entire team and started off the season as the preseason number one team in the country. But the 49ers didn't have the same chemistry, and despite a 30-5 season, they would fall again to Summitt's Vols, who defeated the 49ers in the Elite Eight and went on to win their second national title.

That was the season the 49ers said goodbye to Toler, who would become the third Beach player to have her jersey retired, along with Pollard and Brown. Toler averaged over twenty points per game in her career and set a school record for career assists. She went on to play three seasons in the WNBA, becoming the first player to score a basket in the newly formed league in 1997, when she hit a baseline jumper for the LA Sparks against the New York Liberty. Toler went on to a front-office career as general manager of the Sparks.

The Beach would fall in the second round of the NCAA Tournament each of the next two years before Bonvicini left for Arizona.

The 49ers were routinely beating USC and UCLA—even when the Trojans had top-level talent like Cheryl Miller. But after the Pac-10 added women's sports, it became tough for Bonvicini to compete recruiting-wise with the big football powers.

"The straw that broke the camel's back was Lisa Leslie," says Bonvicini.

BASKETBALL IN LONG BEACH

Joan Bonvicini leaves the floor after the 49ers' 1988 Final Four loss. Press-Telegram *file photo.*

Leslie came to all of the 49ers' camps from her freshman year, and Bonvicini was sure she'd end up in black and gold. But Leslie changed her mind and went to the Trojans. "I could see that things were going to change," Bonvicini says. "The school was a mid-major in other sports but a top ten team in women's basketball—and I wanted to feel like that. I didn't want to watch it go down."

Arizona called Bonvicini on the Monday after a Saturday loss to Georgia in the NCAA Tournament, and she left for the opportunity to coach a Pac-12 school. "It really wasn't the money, it was that opportunity," she says. "Hindsight is twenty-twenty. I took over the worst program in Division I, and it took longer to rebuild than I thought. I loved my time in Long Beach—we were way ahead of what was going on."

The Years Since

The years after Bonvicini departed saw, as she feared, the 49ers' slow slide into irrelevance on the national level. Top recruits routinely picked USC and UCLA, and eventually national powers rose in Tennessee and northern California and on the East Coast.

BASKETBALL IN LONG BEACH

The man who replaced Bonvicini in 1991–92 was a beloved 49er figure, Glenn McDonald, a star for the university's men's team and an assistant under Bonvicini. Just two years after Bonvicini left, in 1992–93, the team had its first losing season after thirty years on the right side of the .500 line. McDonald, Dallas Bola and Mary Hegarty were the team's coaches from 1991 until 2009, with only occasional highlight seasons. Bola's 1999–2000 team went 22-11 and won a pair of WNIT games, but the 49ers never approached their former glory and never made the NCAAs after 1992.

In 2009, athletic director Vic Cegles hired Jody Wynn, a USC assistant, cracking at the press conference, "How could I pass on someone named Wynn?"

While injuries have hampered Wynn's 49ers, there's no doubt that the trajectory has been back up. In 2014–15, the 49ers went 22-10, their first twenty-win season since Bonvicini left, and made the NIT for the second time in three years after a decade-plus absence from postseason play.

With a strong crop of young talent returning and quality recruits signed on for the next few seasons, Wynn hopes to put the Beach back on top.

3
Frank Burlison
Long Beach's Basketball Scribe

Every great story needs a great storyteller, and for four decades, Frank Burlison has chronicled the daily highs and lows of Long Beach hoops.

Burlison has plenty of national significance, as well. He was inducted into the U.S. Basketball Writers Association's Hall of Fame in 2005 and was on the original selection committee for the McDonald's All-American Game. In 1992, *Sports Illustrated* named him one of the ten most influential members of college sports' media. He has covered every NCAA Final Four since 1986 and created the well-respected Best in the West all-star honors.

But to Long Beach hoops fans, Burlison has been a constant, friendly presence at gyms across the city. He got a job as a freelancer for the *Press-Telegram* as a junior at Gahr High in nearby Cerritos, and he never stopped hanging out in gyms.

"I never wanted to play," says Burlison. "I was pragmatic. But when you see something up close, it sort of takes a hold."

Out of high school, he began working for the weekly paper put out by the Olympic Development League and continued stringer work for the *P-T* while attending classes at Long Beach State, where he also covered the school's men's team for the campus paper. After two years of college, the *P-T* made him a relatively unheard-of offer for a writer still two years away from getting his degree: the paper hired him on full time.

"I didn't even finish at Long Beach State because I was working so much," he laughs. "I couldn't turn down the opportunity just for another two years of school. What did I need a journalism degree for? I got my dream job."

BASKETBALL IN LONG BEACH

Burlison continued to spend countless hours in the gyms watching practices and games. When he wasn't in the gym, he was often on the phone for marathon conversations with some of the city's best high school coaches, including Ron Palmer, Bill Odell, Jim Ferguson and Tim Sweeney.

"I learned so much talking to these guys," he says. "Those were the good old days, the glory days—it was an era that doesn't exist anymore."

Long Beach basketball in those days was at its apex, with three Moore League teams making the CIF semifinals at the Long Beach Arena in 1977. But as the glory days receded, Burlison remained, and he's still an encyclopedia of local basketball knowledge, spitting out names, dates and scores almost faster than they can be transcribed.

"We all grew up together," says former Lakewood coach Tim Sweeney. "It was a special time—we were all kids then. Now we see each other and call each other 'old man.'"

Palmer says he was impressed with Burlison from the first time he met him. "He covered us in the Watts games in 1976, and he knew we were going to be good," Palmer remembers. "I still have that story in the archives."

Millikan's Bill Odell gives Burlison even more credit. "The atmosphere in the city at that point, the '70s and '80s, he was a part of that. The promotion he would give and the in-depth analysis. He's a basketball junkie who wasn't a player—he really knows the game."

Over the years, Long Beach's sports fans got to know him, as well, through countless articles and features—a great storyteller for a great story.

4
Pro Basketball in Long Beach and the Summer Pro League

The origin of professional basketball in Long Beach dates back to the Long Beach Elks, a team organized out of the Elks 888 Lodge in the city. Documents suggest it started operating in the early 1930s.

A Theta Chi newsletter from 1932 announces that a graduate of 1931 was playing professional basketball with the Long Beach Elks.

The Elks hosted some of the best Amateur Athletic Union (AAU) teams in the country, including the Phillips 66ers, the premier AAU team in the 1940s. The 66ers won numerous national titles, including six straight from 1943 to 1948.

Long Beach played Phillips on February 21, 1948, at the Municipal Auditorium before a sellout crowd of two thousand. The 66ers crushed the home team 81–26.

Long Beach Chiefs

The city's second chance at a professional basketball team came with the formation of the Long Beach Chiefs in 1962 as part of the fledgling American Basketball League (ABL). The Chiefs originated in Hawaii as the Hawaii Chiefs, an original member of the league under commissioner Abe Saperstein, owner of the Harlem Globetrotters. The ABL was a revolutionary rival league to the NBA, implementing the three-point line and a thirty-second shot clock. Saperstein's formation of the ABL came out of anger; he was upset when the Minneapolis Lakers relocated to Los Angeles after he was promised an LA franchise within the NBA.

Owned by Art Kim, a Hawaii businessman, the Chiefs posted the worst record in the new league and were relocated to Long Beach in July. The jump to the mainland was aided by the folding of the LA Jets midseason after financial issues, leaving a spot open in Southern California.

After the inaugural season, the ABL was trying to fight off rumors that the league would be folding and dealing with issues in the courthouse. The ABL sued the NBA after the NBA tried to add the ABL champion Cleveland Pipers, owned by a young George Steinbrenner, future owner of the New York Yankees.

When Kim addressed the Long Beach media in July, the owner made it clear that the Chiefs were here to stay and not a one-year thing. However, that would not be the case, as the Chiefs did not make it the full 1962–63 season before folding.

Back in Hawaii, the Chiefs were led by head coach Red Rocha, a former center from Oregon State University who went on to play for the Baltimore Bullets and Syracuse Nationals. But Kim decided to go in a different direction, hiring former Wilson Bruin and former Seattle University head coach Al Brightman. Brightman was one of the hottest college coaches in the country after leading Seattle to numerous NCAA Tournament berths and a stunning upset over Saperstein's Globetrotters in 1952. But after a mysterious departure from Seattle following an altercation with John Wooden, Brightman had been struggling to get back into the coaching ranks.

During the 1961 season, Brightman took over coaching the San Francisco Saints, going 23-24, helping him land his new position with Long Beach. Brightman was stocked with some former college all-stars in Bill Spivey (Kentucky), Ron Horn (Indiana), Ben Warley (Tennessee State) and Grady McCollum (Western Illinois).

Yet the financial issues finally caught up with the ABL early into the second season, and the league officially folded on December 31, 1962, catching it by surprise.

"When I arrived in Long Beach, I knew it would take lots of hard work to introduce the people to something new," a stunned Kim told the *Press-Telegram*. "I only regret that my faith in Long Beach was not borne out conclusively because the question of Long Beach's emergence as a major sports center never can be answered by the ABL now."

BASKETBALL IN LONG BEACH

Long Beach Jam

In 1967, a new basketball league was once again started to compete with the NBA: the American Basketball Association, famously known as the ABA. The new league was known as one with exciting offensive showings and stars like Rick Barry, Julius Erving and Spencer Haywood, leading the NBA to eventually relent and merge with the ABA in 1976.

The ABA was no more; that is, until 2000, when the ABA returned, although just in name and not quite in star power. The rebirth brought professional basketball back to Long Beach with the formation of the Long Beach Jam franchise in 2003.

Long Beach's newest pro franchise immediately made a splash by winning the 2004 ABA championship and adding a former NBA superstar to the roster.

The Jam made national headlines with the signing of former Chicago Bulls star and five-time NBA champion Dennis Rodman. The forty-two-year-old Rodman was signed in December but played just two games with the Jam, nursing a knee injury.

The Jam released Rodman two weeks after his signing to allow the former star to try to join an NBA team in need.

It was a long, wild first season for the Jam, formed in May 2003 and named in June. It saw its first coach, Paul Westhead, leave for the NBA after the first regular-season game. Under new head coach Earl Cureton, the Jam overcame five players, including Matt Barnes, getting signed by NBA teams and won the regular-season championship with a 154–117 win over Las Vegas.

Long Beach advanced to the championship game against the defending champions, the Kansas City Knights, with more than three thousand fans filling the Walter Pyramid.

The Jam got a boost heading into the championship with the return of Rodman, who was planning on attending as a fan and instead found himself on the bench.

In a high-scoring affair, Derrick Dial banked in a go-ahead three-pointer with thirty-two seconds left before Geno Carlisle stole the ball for the Jam with seven seconds left to dribble out the clock for the 126–123 win. Rodman famously was not aware that the game was for a championship.

"I wasn't worried about winning a championship because I didn't know that the championship was today," Rodman told the media after the game. "I thought this was the beginning of the playoffs. But this is great anyway."

Yet it seems unlikely that Rodman did not know that it was, in fact, the championship game. The former NBA Defensive Player of the Year was quoted in the Associated Press four days before the championship as saying he was excited for the chance to become the first player to win both an NBA and ABA title.

Long Beach wasn't able to defend its ABA crown the following year after an early exit in the playoffs. The Jam finished in second place in the Red Division behind the Utah Snowbears. As the number eight seed in the playoffs, Long Beach defeated number nine Las Vegas 148–126 before falling by fifteen points to the number one seeded Snowbears.

That would be the last game for the Jam franchise in Long Beach. The team withdrew from the ABA and applied for admission to the National Basketball Development League, commonly known as the D-League. The Jam was granted access for the 2006–07 season and relocated to Bakersfield.

After the Jam departed, the league announced in late 2006 that Long Beach would be getting a new team: the Long Beach Storm. The Storm was slated to begin play in 2007 and owned by Nicole Wainwright, a local business owner. But a late ownership change to Carl Williams resulted in the Storm becoming the Long Beach Breakers.

With former NBA player Olden Polynice as head coach, the Breakers embarked on a 10-7 season, finishing third in the Southwest Division. The Breakers defeated the Maywood Buzz 120–112 in the wild card round before falling to the San Francisco Rumble 129–115. In January, the team announced it was once again moving, this time relocating to Huntington Beach.

Long Beach Stingrays

As a city known for pioneering women's basketball, it only made sense that Long Beach would be home to one of the first women's professional basketball teams in the country.

Unlike the ABA, which was created as a direct challenge the NBA, the American Basketball League (ABL) was formed during the time the NBA was creating the Women's National Basketball Association (WNBA).

The ABL, founded in 1996 with eight clubs, and the WNBA were results of the boom in popularity of women's basketball after the 1996 USA women's Olympic team won the gold medal in Atlanta.

After all eight teams made it through the inaugural season, the ABL decided to expand with the Long Beach Stingrays for the 1997–98 season, playing in the Walter Pyramid and coached by Maura McHugh.

BASKETBALL IN LONG BEACH

McHugh was a star at Old Dominion in the early 1970s, one of the first female athletes to earn an athletic scholarship in the country. McHugh served as the head coach at Oklahoma and Arizona State until 1993, and then took a break from coaching before being called up by the new franchise while living in Arizona, where she was working for a nonprofit organization.

"It was a really fun league to coach in. It was the first time I was in a league that was all about the women," said McHugh. "That's what it was all about. We were the main attraction."

The WNBA was backed by the NBA, but the ABL was described as having a higher quality of play and boasted higher salaries for its players.

"It was a big rivalry between the two leagues," said McHugh. "We were both trying to attract the top players."

Yet what the WNBA did have was better infrastructure, while McHugh and the front office of the ABL struggled to set up everything from scratch for the new franchise.

As the newest member in the fold, the Stingrays were slated to finish last in their inaugural season, but behind number one pick Yolanda Griffith, dubbed the Defensive Player of the Year, and Olympian Venus Lacy, Long Beach finished second in the Western Conference. Griffith, a two-time gold medalist, would go on to become one of the best players in the history of women's basketball, becoming a WNBA Hall of Fame member and an MVP.

In the postseason, the Stingrays advanced to the ABL semifinals after defeating the Colorado Xplosion in the first round series 2–1. Long Beach stunned Portland with a 2–0 sweep, moving on to the championship match with a 70–69 win behind a growing fan base in Long Beach.

Facing the defending champion, the Columbus Quest, the Stingrays jumped to a 2–0 lead in the best-of-five series at the Pyramid.

Yet the Quest responded with two straight wins to set up the deciding Game 5 in Columbus.

The two teams were tied at 33–33 at halftime, but the Quest capitalized on some big three-pointers for a 58–49 lead in the fourth quarter.

The Stingrays made a comeback behind former University of Texas star and two-time Naismith Player of the Year Clarissa Davis-Wrightstil. The future of Hall of Fame member scored thirty-six points in the effort, drilling a three-pointer with 1:32 left on the clock to put Long Beach within one point. However, the Quest made eight of its ten free throws down the stretch to win a second straight title, 86–81.

That five-point loss would go down as the final game in Long Beach Stingrays history. The team would fold unexpectedly six months later.

BASKETBALL IN LONG BEACH

Financial issues with the league were well known; the larger salaries, travel and lack of sponsorships were a worry for teams. On August 26, the Stingrays officially learned that they were no more.

It was a puzzling decision amid the financial troubles since the ABL decided to bring in two more franchises in Chicago and Nashville after folding Long Beach. The ABL never made it a full third season, folding before the league's All-Star game.

McHugh is still confused about why the league decided to add two new franchises and closing down one that nearly won it all.

"It was sad," said McHugh. "We had a good thing going."

Summer Pro League

Ironically, while the city hasn't been able to sustain a pro team due to a lack of interest, it did have a major pro presence for thirteen years in the Summer Pro League (SPL)—one that was lured away from Long Beach because national interest in the event was too high.

The Summer Pro League was started in 1969 as a place for NBA teams to work out their new players. The event never had a true home, bouncing all around Southern California for decades with stops on college campuses at UCLA, Loyola Marymount, Pepperdine and UC Irvine.

Finally, in 1995, after twenty-five years of moving from campus to campus, the SPL landed in the Pyramid at Long Beach State. The reason behind the move was simple, according to SPL co-owner and Laker legend Magic Johnson. He was quoted in the *Press-Telegram* as saying that it was primarily for geographic reasons. "We're excited about playing here—it's right in the middle, between LA and Orange County. It's going to be great for fans all over. The basketball junkies are going to be in heaven."

For thirteen years, they absolutely were. That first year, for example, several NBA teams visited, including the Lakers, Spurs and Suns. Also visiting were national teams from Canada and Mexico, the Harlem Globetrotters and Magic Johnson's All-Stars, a team made up of Johnson and other NBA alums.

Tickets were dirt-cheap. You could watch seven games in a day for eight bucks or get a pass for the entire week the SPL was running for fifty dollars, which would get you into as many as forty-nine games. There were plenty of forgettable contests, sure, between teams made up of NBA hopefuls.

BASKETBALL IN LONG BEACH

The Walter Pyramid at Long Beach State, which since its construction in 1994 has played host to the 49ers, as well as to a few pro teams and, for a number of years, the NBA's Summer Pro League. *Courtesy Stephen Dachman.*

But there was the chance for young fans to catch a glimpse of greats like Magic and to see young players make their debuts. Tracy McGrady, Kevin Garnett, Amare Stoudemire and many others played their first professional games on the court at the Pyramid. The highlight, though, was July 15, 1996, when Kobe Bryant put on a Lakers jersey for the first time and scored twenty-seven points in a game against the Pistons.

The hype surrounding that game was insane, and more than five thousand fans packed into the sold-out Pyramid. At that time, YouTube wasn't yet part of youth basketball, and the only footage that was circulating of the much-hyped seventeen-year-old was a few grainy clips from high school games.

So the line wrapped around the building, and fans crammed in. Bryant didn't disappoint, hitting his first two shots to loud cheers. "I felt very comfortable out there, and I know things will get better," he told the *LA Times* after the game. "I'm happy with my first game."

It was a significant enough night that Bryant and Derek Fisher referenced it during postgame comments after the duo's fifth NBA title together in 2010.

Unfortunately, in 2007, the NBA teams moved up I-15 to Las Vegas, where the city rolled out the red carpet and built a whole month around hosting NBA talent. The games are played in smaller gyms before fewer fans, with significantly less hype and excitement—and in the last sixteen

BASKETBALL IN LONG BEACH

years, nothing regular has come to Long Beach to replace the thrill of seeing future stars for dirt-cheap prices.

That doesn't mean there hasn't been a steady stream of high-profile events. For one, NBA stars have continued to return to the Pyramid for offseason workouts, with DeMar DeRozan, James Harden, John Wall and others playing in closed pickup games.

During the NBA's 2011 lockout, the Pyramid played host to a matchup between the all-stars of the Drew League and the Goodman League, which featured top-level talents like Kevin Durant, Harden, Wall, Brandon Jennings and Rudy Gay. Durant's Thunder teammate Russell Westbrook sat courtside for the 151–144 victory for the Drew League, led by forty-eight points from Harden. The gym was packed floor to ceiling with fans in what might unofficially be the biggest crowd the Pyramid has ever held.

While likely no event in town has ever matched the star power of that game, the BallIsLife All-American high school game held annually at LBCC for the last several years has been a good showcase for up-and-coming talent. For example, Zach LaVine thrilled the sellout crowd at the event's dunk contest—which he won easily—and then went on to win the NBA's dunk contest two years later using the same moves.

So while there may not be a pro presence in Long Beach, the city's central location, as well as its built-in hoops fan base, will always draw big events.

5
LONG BEACH POLY

Long Beach has a number of quality high school basketball programs, but the city also has the state's crown jewel: Long Beach Poly. The Jackrabbits' boys' teams have won twenty CIF championships, lost another fifteen, sent dozens and dozens of players on to the NCAA and have an incredible consistency that is unmatched. Since Poly won its first CIF championship in 1921, it has won at least once every decade since.

At the conclusion of the 2015 season, 110 years into Poly's history, the Jackrabbits' boys' team had won 1,891 games.

The cover of James Heartwell's seminal history of the first fifty years of Poly basketball. *Poly archives.*

BASKETBALL IN LONG BEACH

"It's the winningest program in California history," says Mark Tennis, editor of *Cal-Hi Sports* and a high school sports historian. "They're pretty far ahead of anyone else, and Poly is one of the best places for basketball in the country."

That's to say nothing of Poly's girls' basketball program, which has its own rich legacy of state titles and NCAA talent.

The Jackrabbits' history could easily fill a book of its own, and it has received several in-depth accountings before, including James Heartwell's excellent 50th Anniversary Golden Jubilee history of the program, published in 1954, and Bob Keisser's equally excellent 100th anniversary retrospective in the *Press-Telegram* in 2005. Here is the most comprehensive and in-depth treatment available, a chapter that owes a debt to both of those histories.

The Early Years: 1895–1919

Many have wondered why Poly has been known as a football school rather than as a basketball school, despite the fact that both programs are the most successful in state history; in fact, as of 2015, the Poly boys' basketball team had more CIF championships (twenty) than the football team (nineteen). Throw in six state titles and five CIF rings for the girls' team and it's a legitimate question.

The answer might date back to the very early 1900s, when Poly's boys refused to pick up the round ball for a simple reason: they didn't want to lose to the girls. Early Poly yearbooks chronicle that the first Jackrabbits teams played against each other, with the girls' teams easily defeating the boys. The punishment was harsh for the boys—not only were they mocked by their classmates for losing to a team of girls, but they also had to buy the winning team ice cream as part of the annual bet.

The first season for the Poly boys was in 1904–05, with the first game taking place against the Ermita Athletic Association on November 1, 1904. But the sport wouldn't begin to take root for a few years—for the Poly boys at least. In 1907, the Jackrabbit girls beat the boys 20–14. Basketball developed a nickname at what was then called Long Beach High School: the "sissy sport."

The Poly boys' team would quickly begin developing a few years later, but when the Jackrabbits won the 1909 city championship, led by Lorne

BASKETBALL IN LONG BEACH

The Jackrabbits played outside for their first several seasons before a gym was built. *Poly yearbook.*

Middough and captain Guy Bartow, the school's yearbook noted, "This was practically the first year of boys' basketball. The team was planted about three years ago but has always been neglected in our anxiety to encourage the girls." The Poly boys spent their time practicing against the girls on the outdoor dirt court, which they shared during practice time because the school only had one.

The team won the city championship in 1909 by beating teams from the YMCA, churches and other local organizations, as there weren't yet any other high schools in town. The Jackrabbits then lost in the county league playoffs, which was understandable given that they did not have a coach.

They got their first head coach in 1910, when Roy Coffin took up the task, but were doomed in the league title because a large track meet had been held on campus the day before, and most of the basketball team was "not as fresh as they should have been," according to the yearbook, due to having participated.

The Jackrabbit teams starred the Middough brothers through their early years, with Lorne, Roy and Way all taking turns as the team's leading scorer. Way and Lorne would go on to great things in the city, with Lorne becoming an assemblyman and the two brothers building a historic site downtown at 205 East Broadway. In 1923, they erected the building at a cost of $400,000—it played home to Long Beach's small claims and superior courts in the 1920s, but the bas-relief art around the exterior featured scenes of children playing sports, as both felt that was important in life. They actually included a gymnasium in the building to allow high school students to play and train, although that was done away with when they sold the building in the 1930s.

BASKETBALL IN LONG BEACH

The team operated with a coach on and off, winning the unofficial city title but failing to win county championship playoff series, which at that time weren't yet organized by the CIF (it wasn't founded until 1913). In 1912, it won the county title but lost a playoff series with Huntington Beach; that was the year the Jackrabbits were coached by CM Lyons and starred Way Middough and also the year that the program really began to build. "In former years, there was little interest taken in it by students, but this year there was a good attendance at all the games," says the yearbook.

But the years after would see the yearbook filled with complaints that fans weren't coming out again and explanations for why the team didn't win many games, occasionally dipping under a .500 winning percentage. In 1917, Ed Kienholz took over the team for the season in his first year on campus. He would go on to great coaching success at Poly in both basketball and football after a brief hiatus to fight in World War I.

"I had to begin at the bottom and work up in terms of teaching them a style of play," he said at the time. The team went 3-2 that year but lost the county title in a game at Pasadena, where its opponent's head coach was also the game's referee.

The next two years, Kienholz was overseas fighting, and the Jackrabbits—along with the rest of Southern California—didn't field a team in 1919 due to the influenza epidemic and the war. When Kienholz returned the next year, the Jackrabbits would jump to new heights.

THE HIDDEN DYNASTY

There are no banners hung on the wall for the pre-CIF Poly girls' basketball teams, no numbers representing CIF and state championships. None of the members of those teams or its coach are in a Hall of Fame—but they certainly could be. Prior to the founding of the CIF in 1913, the Jackrabbits were the unquestioned best team in the state, even competing with colleges and routinely beating USC's women's team in their annual contest.

The team began playing in 1906 and was quickly beating the boys' team in the annual contest by a wide margin, driving the boys away from the sport out of embarrassment. The Jackrabbits were coached by Gertrude Upton, a trailblazing figure who led in a full skirt and lace collar, her hair pulled back severely into a tight bun. Not much information about her exists in the Poly records or the newspaper, but one thing is certain: Upton was leading Poly's girls to championships a few years before it was even legal for her to vote. She coached the team for six years, from 1906 to 1911, and the Jackrabbits won their final game of the season each one of those years.

In 1908, Poly's team of Mae Dingman, Mina Taylor, Lily Kingcade, Verna Finklepaugh, Laura Browne and Ethel Howe easily won the championship for the Women's Basketball League of Southern California for the third straight year. It went 7-2, with its only losses to Compton (which it later avenged) and to Colgate College. Poly beat USC in the championship, 13–5.

The next year, 1909, with virtually the entire team returning, the Poly girls won the school's first true state championship. They beat Compton for the SoCal High School and College championship, 13–10. Then they went on to the state playoffs, defeating USC 13–10, setting up a home and home series with Bakersfield High for the state crown.

Girls' Basketball

COACH: Miss Gertrude Upton.

Gertrude Upton, a pioneer and trailblazing girls' basketball coach at Poly in the early 1900s. *Poly yearbook.*

Poly's 1908 girls' basketball team, SoCal champions for a third straight year (and the earliest known photo of a Poly team). *Poly yearbook.*

BASKETBALL IN LONG BEACH

"Bleachers were overflowing long before the time set for the game," reads the yearbook account for the game. Poly didn't have a gymnasium at the time, so all its games were played outside, and the school was known for how well kept its hard-packed dirt courts were. The Jackrabbits were so comfortable there that they actually complained about having to play inside a gymnasium at Bakersfield, where they couldn't feel the ocean breeze.

Poly's 1909 state champion girls' basketball team, the school's first state title team. *Poly yearbook.*

Poly handily beat the Drillers in the game played in Long Beach, which was the first—it won 18–5. The Jackrabbits lost in Bakersfield by two, 11–9, which gave the games an average score of a 14–8 Poly win, giving the title to the Jackrabbits. When the team arrived home, the girls were greeted by the city's Municipal Band as they got off the train, and a rally was held at the auditorium, with speeches made by city officials who had purchased championship pins to give to all the girls, as well as Upton.

"We are sorry to relate that we cannot claim the national or world's championship," says the yearbook account in a bit of chest thumping. "Because there is no team which wishes to compete with us for such."

The next season, Poly's girls celebrated two state wins—yes, they won another SoCal and state championship, but their players and coach also gained full citizenship as the State of California recognized women's right to vote. "Whether it is the result of woman suffrage or not, we do not know," reads the Poly yearbook from 1910. "But we are sure that our girls have done gloriously this year."

For the fifth-straight year, the Jackrabbits won the SoCal title, passing the ball more quickly with each contest and posting scores that were unheard of in the pre–shot clock, pre-three-point-line era. They beat Pasadena 54–5 in their opener and then defeated Santa Monica 61–1. They beat USC 38–11 for the SoCal title and then defeated northern California's Lowell 16–9 for their second-straight state crown.

Verna Tinklepaugh was the team's star forward and its manager, but it also featured a pair of legit post players, almost unheard of for 1910. Esther

BASKETBALL IN LONG BEACH

Dayman was the team's "running center" at six feet tall, and Jean Robinson played "jumping center," towering over the competition at six-four.

Because Long Beach had been settled by midwestern farmers, the city featured more height and strength than many others in Southern California. And those farmers brought their views on women and work; they didn't see women as being unable to exercise or work hard because on their farms, their wives and daughters had to do those things. That's why, in a time when the nation still was hesitant to let women vote—and fifty-seven years before a Boston Marathon organizer worried that the race's first female runner would have her uterus fall out while running—Long Beach was home to tough, hard-fouling girls' hoops players.

And then there was their coach, who fearlessly encouraged competition and passion from her players, devoting hours and hours to coaching while also running the school's Mathematics Department. "As long as Miss Upton remains to coach our teams, we may rest assured that the championship pennants will continue to come to our school," wrote Tinklepaugh in the yearbook.

The next year, 1911, would prove to be Upton's last, but once again, the Jackrabbits won the SoCal and state titles despite heavy rains preventing them from practicing at their regular clip because the court was too muddy. "Other teams may lose and other teams may win, but our teams will win forever," boasts the yearbook. "It makes no difference if it rains eight days out of the week, making basketball practice impossible."

That year, the Jackrabbits starred Tinklepaugh and Myma Taylor after graduating four starters. They went 9-0, beating Covina for the SoCal title and again for the state title. Upton moved on from coaching after that year, although there are no records that still exist to explain why. Poly moved on without her, but the sport soon dried up.

GIRLS' ATHLETIC ASSOCIATION

A yearbook in 1913 claimed that the team couldn't find other schools to play, "largely due to the superstitious awe with which other teams regard our squad," but that wasn't really the problem. The issue was that the CIF was founded that year and very pointedly did not have girls' sports as part of its program. While Long Beach may have been forward thinking about women in athletics, much of the rest of the state and country was not.

BASKETBALL IN LONG BEACH

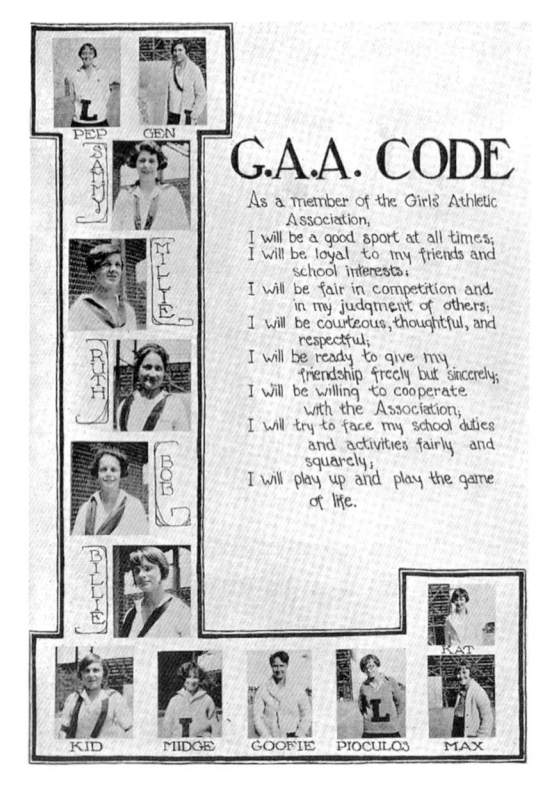

G.A.A. CODE

As a member of the Girls' Athletic Association,
I will be a good sport at all times;
I will be loyal to my friends and school interests;
I will be fair in competition and in my judgment of others;
I will be courteous, thoughtful, and respectful;
I will be ready to give my friendship freely but sincerely;
I will be willing to cooperate with the Association;
I will try to face my school duties and activities fairly and squarely;
I will play up and play the game of life.

After the banning of girls' sports, Poly became one of the first schools in California to form a Girls' Athletic Association. *Poly yearbook.*

Long Beach's parents still wanted their girls playing sports, so even though other schools no longer had teams for the Jackrabbits to play, the school founded the Girls' Student League in 1912, which would later branch off its sports interests as the Girls' Athletic Association. Poly had the first, and best, in the state. The girls on campus played sports, with swimming, tennis, basketball and baseball offered, along with walking.

The contests held on campus were between different classes, with the juniors and seniors playing each other. The competitive spirit was still there, with one game ending in a near-brawl between two classes.

The first president of the Girls' Student League was Hazel Middough, younger sister of the boys' basketball players. In 1915, Middough and the school organized a multiple school carnival that allowed the Jackrabbits to face other schools again, if only for a day.

The shared constitution on which the schools agreed now reads as almost a heartbreaking step backward. Long Beach girls had been encouraged to play hard and rough just a few years prior, but now they endorsed the following philosophy:

> *The purpose of this organization shall be to stand for the ideals of true womanhood: courtesy of speech and manner, simplicity, loyalty, and honor; to aid in all worthy student body activities; to promote the good name of Long Beach High School; and to further the spirit of good fellowship and democracy.*

BASKETBALL IN LONG BEACH

The GSL dropped basketball for a few years when World War I enveloped everyone's attention. In the 1920s, girls' sports flourished again, with interclass games once again serving as the highlight of the athletic year for the Jackrabbit girls. In 1923, the Girls' Athletic Association branched out from the GSL because the interest in sports was high enough to carry its own organization. The Poly GAA remains historically significant for how large and strong it was and how early it developed compared to those at other schools.

The Poly GAA practically rivaled the school's official CIF boys' sports; 115 girls came out for GAA basketball in 1923. Clarinne Llewelyn was the female faculty member who ran the GAA, which featured basketball, track and soccer in its early years. The students developed their own logo and added more sports by the year, including field hockey, tennis, water polo, volleyball, archery and others.

The organization almost came to a gruesome end during the 1933 earthquake that leveled the high school and much of the city. The GAA leadership was walking underneath the school's large dome shortly before the 5:55 p.m. earthquake—had it struck just a minute or two earlier, they would have been crushed.

The GAA continued to operate through the years, taking a brief pause during World War II while the Long Beach high school girls helped with the war effort. When it resumed, it added girls' swimming, with two-piece uniforms causing a brief scandal. The "Bunny Bounce," the interclass basketball tournament, was popular on campus, but Long Beach's high school girls continued to fight for equality while socializing with other high schools in town during GAA "Play Days."

In the 1960s, a pair of Poly legends attended the school, but neither would get to compete for Poly in official varsity sports since GAA action was still all that was available. Tennis legend Billie Jean King and track Hall of Famer Martha Watson were both sports stars while still in their teen years, with Watson making the 1964 Olympics in long jump a few months after graduation and King winning tennis tournaments while still attending classes at Poly.

Watson set a national long jump record while competing in GAA track, but it was obvious that a full sports program was needed, not just in Long Beach but also nationwide. By 1971, the GAA participation at Poly had grown to more than three hundred girls as the women's liberation movement caught fire. Finally, in 1973, in the GAA's fiftieth year of existence on campus, it wasn't needed anymore because of the passage of

BASKETBALL IN LONG BEACH

Title IX, which created equal opportunities for girls and forced the CIF-SS to create a girls' sports program. Soon, the Moore League would be offering girls' sports as well, with Poly led on the court by Cassandra Stipe and Regina Prather in those early years.

It would be a while before Poly was a girls' basketball powerhouse again—but thanks to the Girls' Athletic Association, the sport never died, and Poly girls were always able to play.

Kienholz, Landreth, Church: 1920–1942

The two constants of Poly basketball throughout the years have been strong fundamentals and excellent coaching. That's been the case dating back to the team's first championship team in 1921, a Jackrabbit squad led by legendary Poly football coach Ed Kienholz.

A World War I veteran, Kienholz returned to Long Beach and to his high school job at Poly after the war was over. In 1919–20, his first year back, Poly went 8-2 and won the city and county titles, falling in the championship 27–24 on a muddy outdoor court. The next year, 1921, was one of the best in school history, however, as the Poly boys won one of their two state titles and posted their only undefeated season.

Walter Meyers and Winchell "Bubbles" Boice captained that team and played the two forward spots, while Harry Elcock was center. Glen Hastings and football star Morley Drury were the guards, playing stifling defense. "Only a stiff wind could get by them," read a newspaper account at the time.

The Jackrabbits beat Occidental 59–21 and then handed out a 52–18 defeat to Pomona College and scored a tight 25–15 win over the USC freshman in their closest game of the non-league schedule. After blowing through the Coast League, the "Kienholz machine," as it was dubbed by local papers, headed for the playoffs. It beat Huntington Park 47–17 in the quarterfinals, outscoring its opponents 28–3 in the second half. It steamrolled Ramona 51–15 in the semifinals and then beat Monrovia 36–16 for its first CIF championship. After topping Dinuba 44–24, the team faced Berkeley for the state championship, trying to preserve an undefeated season, the only one in school history.

The game was to take place at the University of California the week after Easter. Kienholz, who knew how to use a sense of humor to balance his hard discipline, got the team together on Easter and had the boys practice shooting

BASKETBALL IN LONG BEACH

Poly's 1921 CIF and state championship boys' team. *Poly yearbook.*

Easter eggs into baskets across the gym. On March 28, Poly played Berkeley and trailed 11–8 at halftime. The Jackrabbits didn't score in the third quarter, but a one-man drive by Hastings up the middle of the court sparked Poly, and it went on to win 21–17 to cap the historic 16-0 state title season.

Keinholz coached another few years to success before stepping away with a career record of 42-10. The program wouldn't get going again until 1927, when another Poly football coaching great, Orian "Toad" Landreth, took over. Landreth won four CIF titles as a football coach at Poly but was just as good a basketball coach.

In his first season, 1927, Poly went 16-1 but lost in the championship game to Huntington Park. The next year, it made it back to the CIF title game but fell again, this time to Santa Monica, 21–17.

Finally, in 1929, Landreth and the Jackrabbits broke through. The team started just 2-2 in non-league but blew through the Coast League undefeated to claim the league title and head into the playoffs with steam, trying to make its third straight championship. Former Jackrabbit star Way Middough came back to give an inspiring speech during a rally, and Poly took heart. The team was captained by Paul Bixby, who led in scoring, and had another good guard in Mark Vail. Bill Voorhees, the center, was exceptional during the playoffs, and the team played airtight defense. It beat Glendale 27–9 after holding Glendale scoreless in the first half.

Finally, Landreth and the Jackrabbits got over the hump in the championship and beat Fullerton, 32–16.

While Kienholz and Landreth were able to give Poly its first two championships, it was Charlie Church who gave the team its first true golden age, taking it to the championship five times during his eleven-year tenure and winning three.

Church, who had previously coached at Wilson, brought a new style and energy to the job, and he coached the team through a pair of tumultuous years. In 1932, his first season, the school was caught up with Olympic fever, with Long Beach hosting rowing and other events. Bob Sandberg, a Poly wrestler who was competing in the Olympics, came and spoke with the team. It made it to the CIF semifinals.

The next year, the campus and city were devastated by the great earthquake of 1933, and Poly won the Coast League title—as well as the first official All-City Championship with a 21–17 win over Wilson—but lost in the first round of the playoffs. The team featured its first black player that year, Walter Ray McCowan, who was also the school's first black football player (he went on to become student body president, the first African American to hold that role at a California high school). There was also a Japanese player and a Jewish player on the team, with Poly's yearbook that year noting the diversity among the team's ranks.

Church's team in 1934 didn't have a regular place to practice since there was no standing gym on campus, and after beating Wilson for the second All-City title, it was defeated by the Bruins, Church's former team, in the playoffs.

Finally, in 1935, Poly made the CIF game—but lost, 20–17, to Santa Barbara at Whittier College, despite fine play from Harold Hofman. He and Bill Moffitt both went that entire season without missing a free throw.

In 1939, Church broke through and won his first CIF championship with the school, capping a 21-3 season. The Jackrabbits beat Whittier 29–17, led by the phenomenal post player Bob Howard, the first-ever CIF Player of the Year, along with talents like Ed Gillean and the Cohee brothers, R.L. and Dave. Howard and the Cohees would go on to undefeated seasons at LBCC, and Howard remained in Long Beach for his entire life, until his recent passing at age ninety, serving as a lifelong coach, teacher and athletic director at Lynwood High. He actually gave future Poly coaching great Carl Buggs his first job shortly before Buggs was going to pack his things and move back home to Oakland.

In a 2004 interview with Bob Keisser, Howard looked back on his time with Coach Church. "Charlie was a great coach," he said. "Very strict, and he taught fundamentals. Most of the coaches since him were the same way—Del Walker, Bill Mulligan, Ron Palmer."

One former Church player, Claude Jennings, said Church would occasionally call 7:00 a.m. practices in a freezing gym to make sure the

Jackrabbits got their running in. "Charlie never used profanity," Jennings told Keisser. "He didn't smoke or chew tobacco. I don't imagine he drank, either. He was a disciplinarian who expected his players to keep their hair short." But Church was also such a good coach that Jennings once got a phone call from an assistant to Jerry Tarkanian during Tark's years at Long Beach State. The assistant wanted to know if Jennings still had Church's old playbooks.

Poly barely made the playoffs in '39—it beat San Diego Hoover 30–22 to nab a Coast League co-championship but then lost a one-game playoff with the same team to decide who went to the playoffs. Fortunately for Poly, Hoover ended up dropping out of the playoffs before they started since two of its players graduated mid-year, right before they began.

Poly was bolstered by a sixth-straight All-City win over Wilson in the newly renovated Municipal Auditorium, in a game the newspapers heralded as the "Civil War," with 2,300 fans crammed into the building. The Jackrabbits won 29–21 and rocketed into the playoffs, winning every game but one by double digits. In the championship, they faced defending CIF champion Whittier and prevailed, 29–17.

The next year, 1940, they picked up where they left off, with Gillean winning CIF Player of the Year. Poly capped the season by beating future Moore League rival Compton 32–19 in a game the Jackrabbits hosted.

Church faced a challenge in 1941, having graduated his entire team, but he still guided Poly to the championship game, where the team, led by Warren McCary and Dick West, lost the title. The next year, Church would cap his tenure with a fourth-straight CIF championship appearance, this time winning against Compton 31–21.

After that, Church stepped away, concluding a twelve-year career that saw him guide Poly to a 202-59 record overall. In his final four years, the Jackrabbits went 82-10, making four-straight CIF title appearances and winning three.

Walker, Mulligan, Foerster: 1943–1973

The Jackrabbits continued to win All-City titles throughout the 1940s but didn't reach the semifinals of the playoffs again until 1951, when they were defeated by Alhambra. Del Walker took over the team that year and returned the Jackrabbits to prominence in the Southland.

BASKETBALL IN LONG BEACH

"The program wasn't as strong coming out of the war," Walker told Bob Keisser for the *Press-Telegram*'s one-hundred-year history of the team. "But we were very well-supported...the kids who came to Poly believed they would play for championships. Their brothers or parents had gone to Poly. It's what everyone expected."

They made it back to the championship in 1954, led by James Smith and Jack Kirkpatrick, who at that time were the top scorers in school history. It was two years later that they claimed the top prize again, with Walker coaching.

"Poly's varsity started the season like the proverbial lamb and ended like the lion," reads the 1956 yearbook account of the championship. Poly lost a few non-league games and opened 2-3 but went 13-1 in the Coast League, losing only a 49–46 overtime contest with Compton.

Part of the reason for the boost was the continued development of a longstanding Poly tradition: football players coming out for basketball. As football season stretched further into the year, it began to take a little longer for the gridiron players to materialize.

The '56 Jackrabbits were stacked, with CIF Co-Player of the Year Jim Hanna bolstered by the presence of Henry Wallace and John "Lefty" Atkinson, whose son, John Jr., would win at Poly twenty-five years later, making them the first father-son duo to win titles at the same school in

Poly's 1956 CIF championship team with super fan Pop Hyde. *Poly yearbook.*

the same sport. Poly prevailed against Montebello 74–63 to claim the championship, capping a 27-5 season.

"That was my best team, better than the 1954 team," Walker told *Press-Telegram* legend John Dixon. "We won all our games by 20 points or more…we used all 17 of our players."

After eight seasons and a 153-65 record, Walker gave way to Howard Lyon, who would go on to great success at Millikan, where the gym is named after him. The man who got the Jackrabbits really going and put his stamp

Aron Carmichael in 1959. Press-Telegram *file photo*.

on the era was Bill Mulligan, a detail-oriented coach who took the team to three championships in six years, winning two.

"I knew the team had won a CIF title and had a lot of great players," Mulligan told Keisser about arriving at Poly. "But you couldn't possibly realize what a big deal it was until you were there for awhile. You were expected to do well."

After losing the first Moore League title when the league was created in 1957–58, the Jackrabbits won four titles under Lyon and Mulligan, with football stars like Dee Andrews and Willie Brown leading the way, along with a star center in Aron Carmichael.

In 1960, Poly lost its first Moore League game to Wilson and then rattled off fourteen-straight wins for Mulligan. Once again, football players like Willie Brown and Harvey Crow pitched in, with All-City Player of the Year Tom Sisk leading the way and John Rambo contributing, as well, before going on to a legendary career in the high jump. BJ Evans and Leddy Baker formed a formidable frontcourt, and Poly steamed into the playoffs, upsetting top-seeded Helix 50–48 in the quarterfinals. Four of Poly's five playoff wins were by single digits, as it proved that Mulligan's defense could win even without overwhelming talent. Poly claimed the CIF title after a 46–39 win over Anaheim in the championship, with Mulligan getting a much-deserved Coach of the Year award from the CIF.

The Tarbabes of Compton got Poly back in the championship game the next year, ending John Rambo, Leddy Baker and BJ Evans's season 57–49 in an all–Moore League championship matchup that saw Poly defeat Jordan in the semifinals. Over the next two years, Mulligan hit a relative dry spell, as Poly didn't play for a championship in either season.

In 1964, though, he pushed the team to new heights as it went 32-1 to start a streak of three straight appearances in the championship game. Gene Washington, the football star, was happy to compete on the hard court and claim the championship he and his football teammates were robbed of in the fall after they were disqualified from the CIF playoffs for watching game film of an opponent.

Trent Gaines began his excellent career at Poly alongside great teammates like Mel Reed and Billy Richards. They led Poly into the championship against St. Pius X and ended up winning a nail-biter 60–58.

Willard Foerster took over the coaching reins from Mulligan in 1965, but the Jackrabbits were a well-oiled machine at that point and blew through the season, going 29-3. Poly's offense was suddenly the story, with Gaines and Washington pitching in and Moore League Player of the Year Chuck

BASKETBALL IN LONG BEACH

Above: The Jackrabbits' 1963 CIF championship team. *Poly yearbook*.

Right: Rich Payne missed this shot, and Poly would go on to lose the 1966 CIF title game 61–60. *Poly yearbook*.

Moore leading the way, along with Mack Calvin, who would go on to an all-conference career at USC and fourteen years of pro basketball, seven in the ABA and seven in the NBA.

Foerster's theme for the year was "no man is an island," and he had Poly playing a hellaciously entertaining brand of basketball, as it set a Moore League record by beating Downey 108–54 and then smashed North Torrance 90–48 in the championship game—at the time the highest score and largest margin in a championship game.

The next year, Poly broke its own Moore League record by beating Costa Mesa 109–81, but despite Co-CIF Player of the Year performances from Moore and Gaines and a 30-2 season, it fell short of the championship in a heartbreaking 61–60 loss to Sierra. From that point on, the Jackrabbits were still competitive and still winning Moore League titles but did not reach the CIF semifinals, even with fine players like Tony Hill and Dale Dillon; that is, until the school made the excellent decision to hire Ron Palmer.

The Ron Palmer Era: 1974–2003

Ron Palmer is not the tallest coach in Long Beach basketball history or the loudest, yet he's the one who commands the most attention. The most successful coach in Long Beach basketball history said before his first season that "no one had high expectations for us this year." With no returning starters and no time to organize summer workouts, Poly went 16-10 overall and just 3-7 in the Moore League.

Palmer was a fundamentals-oriented coach who quickly turned the Poly program around and shaped it into a California powerhouse for the better part of three decades.

"Ron Palmer—very quiet, a little aloof," says Long Beach basketball writer Frank Burlison. "A lot of people thought he was arrogant, but he was opinionated about the game and how it should be played. I learned so much from him. College coaches would say when they got his guys that they didn't have to teach them; they were already so well versed in the fundamentals."

Palmer came to Poly from Pasadena High School, where he famously discovered Michael Cooper and brought him into organized basketball for the first time. Palmer was the JV coach of the Pasadena program and coached track, as well. A student of John Wooden, he believed in the

BASKETBALL IN LONG BEACH

Ron Palmer, legendary Poly coach. Press-Telegram *file photo*.

importance of footwork, balance and ball handling—simple things that made great basketball players.

Palmer interviewed at Poly and was told on the spot that he got the job. When he got back to Pasadena, he was told they were offering him the head track job, so he called Poly and said he wasn't going to take the position. "I loved track. I went to Oregon State on a long jump scholarship," says Palmer, who qualified for the 1960 Olympic Trials. But after thinking it over on the weekend, it bothered Palmer that Pasadena had waited till he had another offer to give him the job. So he called Ed Nichols at Poly and said, "I'm coming."

Palmer had long admired the athletic talent in Long Beach and said he felt blessed when he got into town. "You don't have to be a genius to teach fundamentals," he says. "And it works—I'm not guessing. I know. We struggled for our first year, but by our second year, we were starting to show some results. We took off."

It didn't take long for him to turn things around, with Michael Wiley and Johnny Nash bringing the talent up tremendously in 1975, a year that saw Poly, Jordan, Wilson and Lakewood all ranked in the top ten in the CIF. Poly fell in the quarterfinals, but Nash and Wiley, both juniors, vowed to get the championship the next year—and they did.

In Palmer's third year as head coach at Poly, 1976, he firmly established his legacy with a championship win, with both Nash and Wiley named All-Americans and co-CIF Players of the Year. It didn't hurt to have Tony Gwynn, James Hughes and Clyde Johnson in support as Poly trounced Buena 69–50 for the title. Nash, Wiley and Gwynn would all be NBA draftees, although obviously Gwynn opted for baseball.

"My first day with the team, it was clear that we would play for a championship," Gwynn said to Keisser. "My first exposure to this wasn't even in a game. We had a scrimmage against Inglewood and Reggie Theus, and [Ron Palmer] sent me out to guard him. Here I was, a tenth grader, guarding a guy who was six-six. I didn't know why. What I learned was that he expected me to be able to guard players who were that good."

Gwynn would also say, "I learned most of what I know about sports because of Coach Palmer."

Nash and Wiley were among the best players in city history, with Nash going on to star at Arizona State and Wiley opting for Long Beach State, where he started as a freshman, before going on to play for the Spurs and Clippers in the NBA.

That was the golden era of Moore League basketball, with three Moore League teams playing in the CIF semifinals at the Long Beach Arena in 1977, and three to four routinely ranked in the CIF's top ten for the better part of the decade.

"That was the apex," says Burlison. "The coaching was phenomenal. It was the good old days; it was the glory days. It was an era that doesn't exist anymore. Coaches were all on campus, guys didn't transfer—you almost never saw a sophomore on varsity in the '70s and '80s."

Palmer agrees and says the gauntlet of the Moore League helped sharpen his Jackrabbits. "I can recall games where we would make two mistakes and lose," he says.

Poly made it out of that almost all–Moore League semifinal round and got back in the championship in 1977 at the Long Beach Arena, but despite 178 assists on the season from future Major League Baseball Hall of Famer Tony Gwynn, it fell short in the end, losing to Pasadena. The Moore League at that time was so strong that Poly made it to the championship despite a third-place finish in the league. It lost again in the championship in 1979 and '80, with talented players like James McDonald, Ray Whiting, Ben McDonald (who played for the Cavaliers and Warriors in the NBA) and Ozell Jones (who went on to play for the Spurs and Clippers).

Burlison says the star-studded '79 team that lost the championship was the best Poly team to not win a title.

One thing that helped spur the Poly improvement under Palmer was a key innovation: film. A young man named John Gean taped Poly's practices and games starting in the 1970s, and Palmer would use that film to review mistakes.

"When I got there, they were just running up and down the floor trying to win with athleticism. We pointed out weaknesses and put in a structure, but John Gean was a big part of that," recalls Palmer. Gean, who still films games for the team, started a practice that is now almost universal among high school basketball teams.

"A lot of tradition started at Poly," says Palmer.

Finally, in the winter of 1981, following the school's first CIF football championship in over two decades, basketball did its part to make it a memorable year when Palmer got CIF title number two following two-straight CIF title game defeats.

The team had three preseason All-Americans in Troy Carmon, Kent Seymour and Darrell Patterson; along with John Atkinson and Leroy Washington, it was stacked. But despite plenty of memorable moments, all anyone wants to talk about from that year is the championship game.

Poly was playing San Marcos, which was ranked number one (Poly was number two), in what promised to be a battle of the titans at the LA Sports Arena. The Jackrabbits had been defeated by San Marcos in the title game two years earlier and had lost two close championships in a row headed into the game, facing an undefeated San Marcos team whose five starters had been playing and starting together for three years.

San Marcos led 23–16 after the first quarter and 36–31 at the half, which ended on Atkinson hitting a CIF-record ninety-two-foot buzzer beater. He recalls that he tried the shot only because the weekend before he'd seen an NCAA Tournament game in which a player from Arkansas had made one. Because this was the pre-three-point era, the miracle shot was worth only two points.

"That gave us a tiny bit of momentum, but they were whooping our ass," says Atkinson. "Coach Palmer never raised his voice. He just kept saying, 'Keep playing, we're fine.'"

Poly trailed by twelve points with three minutes left, and Palmer put on a half-court trap and a full-court press that was executed to perfection by his team.

BASKETBALL IN LONG BEACH

"Our full-court press changed that game," remembers Palmer. "The kids stopped that clock, so time just kind of extended—a two-minute game became a five-minute game because they were diving for loose balls."

That effort came from a grounding in fundamentals. "We did a drill every day where he would roll the ball to the free throw line, and we had to pick it up running and dribble it," remembers Atkinson. "We thought it was the dumbest thing. Well, sure enough, there was a loose ball, and Chris Gwynn picked it up in stride while it was rolling and layed it in—most people would have traveled."

With forty-five seconds left, Gwynn's bucket tied the game at sixty-three—then Washington got a steal and scored the game-winner with just over a second left.

"They got a shot off after that, and I could have sworn it was going in," says Palmer, still sounding relieved thirty years later.

"It's the greatest comeback I've ever seen," says Burlison. "When it was over, I remember sitting there with bodies catapulting over me to rush the court. It was incredible—Poly had to do everything right for three minutes, and they did it."

The crowd had been heavily depleted by fans who had left early assuming Palmer was going to have another close CIF loss. Atkinson said a friend of his had to inform his mom that she had left early from one of the greatest comebacks in California history. The students were still there in force. "They said, 'Please stay off the court,' and our guys didn't care," laughs Atkinson. "They all rushed the court."

The energy on campus was unreal, with Poly coming off a football championship that fall—its first in twenty-one years. Atkinson got the keys to assistant coach Erroll Parker's house after the game, with the instructions that he and a few friends could go there and relax while Parker was out on a date.

"When I put the word out that I had keys, the whole block was full of cars and kids—there wasn't even anywhere else to park," Atkinson remembers. "Well, Coach Parker's girlfriend got the idea to cruise by and check it out, and when he got back, the whole street was full. He grabbed me and said, 'What the hell are you doing?' I said, 'It's a party coach, come on in.'"

The Jackrabbits missed the CIF title game in 1982—the only time they didn't make it from 1978 to 1984. They were back in '83, losing to Mater Dei and setting the stage for a year that nobody in Long Beach will ever forget.

The 1984 Poly team is probably the most successful Jackrabbit basketball team ever; it won one of just two state titles in Poly boys' history and was

BASKETBALL IN LONG BEACH

Chris Sandle, Phi Slamma Jamma in 1984. *Poly yearbook*.

crowned national champion by *USA Today* following its 31-2 campaign, led by All-American Chris Sandle and backed up by studs like Terry Stallworth, Reggie Leonard, Vincent Camper and, of course, Morlon Wiley, who played for the Mavericks, Magic, Spurs and Hawks during a twelve-year journeyman pro career. These high-flying players put on their own version of the Phi Slamma Jamma fraternity, thrilling crowds as they racked up win after win. Sandle was one of the top players in Long Beach history, going on to Arizona State and UTEP.

The Jackrabbits beat Mater Dei 45–44 in overtime in another crazy CIF championship game, after Stallworth blocked what would have been a game-winner for the Monarchs to seal the win for Poly. "That was a great championship, a nut-cutter," says Burlison.

"Chris Sandle was the difference, and I always knew he would be," says Palmer. "We played them to the last shot and won the game."

Before the team took off for Oakland for the state title, the city bid it farewell. "There will be a rousing pep rally at noon today," wrote Robin Hinch in the *Press-Telegram*. "At the bang of dawn Saturday, busloads, carloads and planeloads of Poly fans will take off for Oakland to watch their classmates fight for the state championship."

The Jackrabbits went on to easily beat St. Ignatius 65–45 for the state championship, following a one-point win over Crenshaw in the state semifinal. After that year, Palmer's record stood at 271-51 over eleven years, with seven CIF championship appearances.

The aim for all of 1984 was to win the state title, as Morlon Wiley told Keisser. "There just was an expectation level," he said. "We had an attitude of state or bust. Every time we broke a huddle, we'd holler, 'State!'"

For the next four years, Poly was without Palmer, as he took the head-coaching job at Long Beach State. "I didn't apply. They called and offered," he says. His tenure was a long slog through bureaucratic disasters, including a gym whose renovation forced him to hold practices in the morning with half his team and then in the afternoon with the other half.

Chris Kinder took over coaching duties at Poly, with Vincent Camper leading the "Live Five" into 1985, winning the school's eleventh-straight Moore League title. Although Kinder kept the Jackrabbits going with a quarterfinal appearance his first year, for the next three seasons they hovered around .500, with some local talent opting to join Poly alum Tim Sweeney at Lakewood. When Poly went 12-12 in '87 and then 12-13 in 1988, it bottomed out, with its first losing record since 1949 and the first and only consecutive non-winning seasons in school history.

"Chris was a good guy, but it was almost like replacing John Wooden or Dean Smith or anyone that's great," says Burlison. "It's an impossible task."

Then, after Palmer left Long Beach State, the coach decided to make a triumphant return and retook the reins in the 1989–90 season. "I decided to

BASKETBALL IN LONG BEACH

Palmer's triumphant return to Poly from Long Beach State. *Press-Telegram archives.*

go back to Poly. I wouldn't lose any years on my pension. I could take care of my family—that was a great decision," Palmer says.

And oh, what a difference he made! Poly went from 15-12 the season before to a 28-3 juggernaut in the 1990 playoffs under Palmer, winning a CIF championship thanks to yet another nail-biter, this time 60–58 over Lynwood, after defeating Lakewood in the semifinals. The Jackrabbits were certainly not hurting for talent, with Rod Hannibal and future NFL great Willie McGinest. A young Tyus Edney bolstered the team, as did Sharrief Metoyer, who would return to Poly as a coach.

Edney, an electrifying point guard, went on to star at UCLA, where he had a Hall of Fame career, winning the Francis Pomeroy Naismith Trophy (for the nation's top player under six feet tall), and cemented his legacy for all time with a famous court-to-court game-winner in the second round of the NCAA Tournament in '95 (shown every year as part of the March Madness montages). He was a national champion as a Bruin. Edney had a sixteen-year pro career, including three years in the NBA with the Kings and Celtics. In 2010, he began a coaching career at UCLA.

"We really only had six kids on that team, which was unique," says Palmer. "The biggest impediment we had to overcome was that Tyus was a junior,

BASKETBALL IN LONG BEACH

Poly's 1994 CIF championship team. *Poly archives.*

and the others were seniors. We had to convince them the ball belonged in his hands. Once we did that, we were OK."

Palmer's second act was arguably better than his first, as he won five championships (and lost three more) in his final thirteen seasons with the Jackrabbits. In 1994, they claimed the crown again with a 71–60 win over Crescenta Valley, with Zerrick Campbell and James Brown leading the way. In '95, they lost the championship, and the next year they failed to win a playoff game for one of just two times in Palmer's career.

In '97, though, Poly—led by Rickey Anderson, Mike McDonald and Leland Mathews—beat Miller 63–53. The next two years live in infamy as Poly was defeated by Artesia in both championship games, but the Pioneers later vacated all their wins from both seasons following an investigation that unveiled multiple illegal recruiting infractions by the school. Although Poly was clearly the best team in the CIF that was competing legally, those championships weren't awarded to the Jackrabbits but rather left vacant, with Rickey Anderson, Wesley Stokes and Shea Anderson ending their seasons empty-handed.

That's something that still bothers Palmer. "In my opinion, those championships should be given to the school. We did everything above board," he says. "They weren't playing honestly, and we were. I resent that. We did it the way it was supposed to be done, and we deserve those championships."

BASKETBALL IN LONG BEACH

In the year 2000, Palmer's Jackrabbits made their fourth-straight CIF championship appearance, this time fighting against an opponent who wasn't cheating. They won, beating Ayala 47–35. Stokes, with his wicked crossover, was named All-CIF along with Joe Travis. The team featured a scrappy guard named AJ Diggs who would go on to play at Cal and then figure prominently as an assistant coach under Metoyer. In 2000, Poly was 31-3 and one of the best teams the school had seen—although it fell in the state semifinals.

The Jackrabbits were back in the CIF championship in 2002, when they defeated Eisenhower 64–53, led by CIF Player of the Year Bobby Jones and All-CIF Reggie Butler. James McDonald Jr. went on to an MLB career, Mercedes Lewis to a Pro Bowl NFL career and Winston Justice to an NFL career as well. Poly was 30-4 that season but lost the CIF State SoCal Final to Westchester. Palmer's Jackrabbits went 20-8 the next season, and he called it a career. What a career it was!

In twenty-six years of coaching the Jackrabbits, he won 601 games and went to the CIF finals an astounding fifteen times, winning eight rings. He sent fifty-four players on to play college basketball on scholarship, with others like McGinest and Lewis accepting football scholarships instead. Five of his players went on to the NBA. His legacy is unmatched by any other coach in Long Beach or Southern California history. Not long after his retirement, Poly named its gym the Ron Palmer Pavilion.

SHARRIEF METOYER, SHELTON DIGGS: 2004–PRESENT

"It was important to me and satisfying to pass the job to Sharrief," says Palmer.

Since Palmer's hiring in 1974, the Jackrabbits have had an unbroken line of coaches, with two of his former players coming back to take the reins. Sharrief Metoyer coached from 2004 to 2013, and Shelton Diggs took over after that. Throw in the fact that Palmer's longtime assistant Erroll Parker (whom Palmer calls a "catalyst") has remained a guiding figure and the presence of former Palmer players John Atkinson Jr. and AJ Diggs and it's easy to understand why the coaches talk about the "Poly Way."

The Poly Way is accountability, hard-nosed defense and skilled execution. Both Metoyer and Diggs are quick to reference their high school coach's way of doing things, and both have also enjoyed great success in running the Jackrabbits. That's not a surprise for a school known for its quality coaches—with the exception of Kinder's brief tenure, the last person to coach Poly who didn't win a CIF title was Kenny Welch, who ran the team from 1944 to 1947.

Metoyer was a natural fit to take over for Palmer; not only had he played for the legendary coach, but he was also a strong proponent of Palmer's defense-first, disciplined style of coaching. The Jackrabbits had immediate success under Metoyer, winning the CIF championship in 2004 against Etiwanda, 50–34, led by Chris Fields and Marcus Lewis. The Jackrabbits would play Etiwanda several years in a row in the postseason during Metoyer's tenure.

"One of the biggest things about that year for me was that I had been on Palmer's staff for five years and had grown with those kids, particularly Marcus Lewis and Chris Fields," says Metoyer. "So I had to separate myself from being the young assistant to now being the head coach. I think it helped that coach Palmer moved away, so he wasn't looking over my shoulder. I didn't feel that pressure."

Poly suffered an early setback with a thirty-nine-point loss to Dominguez, which it would avenge later in a game that served as a turning point for the year. Metoyer says he felt it was a smooth transition from the Ron Palmer era. "I never went away from what I learned from him—that was the value in me not only playing for him but me coaching with him," he says.

"It was a smooth transition because Sharrief philosophically had been influenced so heavily by Palmer," says Burlison. "And for the most part, he coached like Palmer did."

Chris Fields was co-CIF Player of the Year for the '04 season along with Etiwanda's Darren Collison. The Jackrabbits remained a talented team but faltered for a few seasons, before Metoyer really built the program back up toward the end of the decade, culminating in a 2011 team that was one of the best in school history. Poly had a core quartet of seniors in Ryan Anderson, Alexis Moore, Alex Carmon and Chris Camper, who had been starting together since their sophomore year. Anderson would end up at Arizona, and Moore signed with USC out of high school. Carmon's father, Troy, won a CIF title in 1981, along with teammate and 2011 assistant coach John Atkinson Jr., highlighting the depth of Poly's tradition.

Added to that quartet was sophomore Roschon Prince, who would go on to become the school's leading career scorer, a PARADE All-American and the Gatorade State Player of the Year.

In 2011, the Jackrabbits went 31-2 and finished ranked number five in the nation, winning an easy CIF championship over Corona Centennial, 68–52.

BASKETBALL IN LONG BEACH

Roschon Prince goes up for a dunk. The All-American set a new career scoring mark for the Jackrabbits before going on to a career at USC and Long Beach State. *Courtesy William Johnson.*

They would play in the title game again the next year in what was expected to be a rebuilding year, although they fell short. The 2012–13 season was one of the most anticipated in school history, and it ended up being notable for totally unexpected reasons.

In addition to Prince, fully developed in his senior year, Poly also featured Jordan Bell, a dynamic athlete who went on to shatter Oregon's records for blocked shots as a freshman. The team had transfer Kameron Chatman as well, giving it three of the top players in the nation.

But before the season started, the CIF ruled Chatman ineligible because Metoyer had coached him on a club team the previous summer. The episode became a protracted, ugly affair, with Metoyer and many Poly fans feeling slighted by the CIF. No other player in the CIF Southern Section was held out as ineligible for the entirety of that season.

BASKETBALL IN LONG BEACH

Sharrief Metoyer during the infamous 2013 state playoff game, when he inserted an ineligible player resulting in a one-year suspension. *Courtesy Stephen Dachman.*

Poly still had a great season with Prince and Bell leading the way and a sophomore point guard named KJ Feagin reminding some of a young Tyus Edney. It finished 28-4 and ranked number eighteen in the nation, but it didn't make it to the championship after Etiwanda eliminated it in the semifinals of the CIF playoffs. After qualifying for state, Poly found itself on the road against longtime rival Mater Dei.

When the result of the game was obvious, with the Monarchs set to prevail, Metoyer made the decision to insert the ineligible Chatman into the game as an act of protest.

Not surprisingly, both the CIF and the CIF state office took it as the affront that it was. The punishment was harsh: Metoyer was suspended for a full season.

Metoyer's former coach was saddened to hear what had happened. "I thought, sometimes you make a bad decision," Palmer says. "The CIF is relentless. They are not going to tolerate something like that. I'm pretty sure if he had that decision to make over again, he'd reverse it."

BASKETBALL IN LONG BEACH

Atkinson, one of Metoyer's assistants, echoed Palmer's thoughts. "It really bothered him all year, that it was taken from that kid," he says. "I think if he had to do it again, he'd do it differently. Palmer actually told me it was my fault—that it was the assistant coach's job to make sure the coach doesn't get in trouble. And I didn't stop him."

Metoyer says, "My perspective on it hasn't changed much. I still think what happened to Kameron was unfair and unjust, specifically because of how the section ruled in other cases. It is what it is. I did what I did, and I don't regret it."

Chatman ended up at Michigan and Prince at USC before transferring to Long Beach State. With Bell starring at Oregon, it's hard for local basketball fans not to wonder about what may have been the greatest Long Beach team that never was.

Poly in those years posted one of the most dominant Moore League stretches in city history. "Between 2011 and 2013, our average margin of victory in the league was almost thirty-five points per game," says Metoyer. "That's never been done."

Shelton Diggs celebrates the Jackrabbits' 2014 Pac Shores championship, which came in his first year as head coach. *Courtesy Thomas Cordova.*

The man who was appointed to the interim coach position during Metoyer's suspension was Shelton Diggs, a Jackrabbit who played for Palmer and the older brother of Metoyer's assistant, AJ Diggs.

Shelton Diggs was well grounded in the Poly Way and had been helping run Poly's lower-level team and scouting for varsity. Diggs started off his career with a bang in 2014, winning the program's twentieth CIF championship in his first season, with Feagin winning CIF Player of the Year honors.

At the conclusion of his suspension, Metoyer opted not to return, although he continues to coach elite club programs. Shelton Diggs was named head coach at Poly—without the interim tag—almost immediately after. Given that he'd won a title in his first year, it was a natural choice.

"That was the easiest hire I'll ever make in my life," joked Poly athletic director Rob Shock.

Top Players

One tradition through the decades is reporters asking coaches to name their top players. Del Walker volunteered that Jim Hanna (USC) and Bob Blake (California) were his two best, while Charlie Church told Jim Heartwell (for his fifty-year retrospective) that Frank Maher was his best all-around player, although he didn't get the acclaim that Bob Howard did. The only coach who regularly declines to talk about his best players is the one people would be most curious to hear from, but Ron Palmer maintains he doesn't want to slight anyone. Burlison, though, says the top players he saw from Palmer's era were the Wileys, Johnny Nash, Tyus Edney, James McDonald, Chris Sandle and Tony Gwynn.

Metoyer thought on it and chose for his top five: Marcus Lewis and Chris Fields from his first championship team and Ryan Anderson, Roschon Prince and Alexis Moore from his later seasons.

The Rise of the Jackrabbit Girls

The Poly girls' team hit some speed bumps on its way back to prominence. In the early Title IX years in the 1970s, Sue Barker coached the girls to several Moore League titles and a CIF championship berth in 1980, when the Jackrabbits were defeated by Cheryl Miller's Riverside Poly team, 64–48.

In the early 1990s, Ed Gaffney took over, but he passed away suddenly in the summer before the 1994 season, and Stephanie Bassard took over. The Jackrabbits won a co–Moore League title with Millikan that year but then claimed the CIF championship in 1995, the first "official" one for the Jackrabbits since their early success predated the CIF. They went 21-4 that year and beat Peninsula for the title, led by four-year starting point guard KK Johns, Sarah Cherin, Kanesha Sanders and Ovana Wallace.

The team's future coach Carl Buggs had arrived on campus that year to coach volleyball and remembers being impressed with Johns. "I didn't know anything about the girls' basketball program, but my office was near the girls' gym. My first day at school, KK was the first person I met. She was there early in the morning with a basketball in her hand. She knew I'd just gotten hired, and she said, 'Hi, welcome to Poly. We're going to win a CIF championship. Those were the first words out of her mouth."

It became a daily ritual. Johns would remind Buggs every day—just as she reminded several people on campus—and sure enough, she got it done. The program struggled until Buggs was hired for the 1999–2000 season, ushering in a new era of Jackrabbit dominance.

Carl Buggs

Almost as impressive as the new heights that the Jackrabbits have reached in the last decade is how close they came to not getting there. If not for several tiny twists and turns, it certainly could have turned out that way.

Carl Buggs came down to Long Beach to be a Dirtbag, playing baseball at Long Beach State. The Oakland native worked for the 49er youth camps after graduation but was running low on money while looking for a teaching and coaching job and was on the brink of moving back to Oakland when he ended up getting a job from Bob Howard, the former Poly CIF Player of the Year in 1939, over at Lynwood High.

Buggs was happy to stay in Southern California and, several years later, opted to take the job coaching volleyball at Poly. He had no aspirations to coach basketball; in fact, he actively wanted to avoid it, although his wife, Lakeisha, was an assistant for the team.

BASKETBALL IN LONG BEACH

"When the job opened up [in 1999], I didn't apply," says Buggs. He was in the middle of the boys' volleyball playoffs at the time and was enjoying a successful run as the coach of that program. There were twenty applicants and three finalists, but the process dragged on long enough that two of the finalists had taken other jobs, and the third, Millikan and UCLA grad Nickey Hilbert, decided to withdraw.

So, with its back against the wall, the administration approached Buggs. Poly principal Shawn Ashley asked for a meeting with him in the middle of the volleyball playoffs and asked what it would take. "I said I'll do it for one year, but I don't want to give up volleyball, so I need a conference and a coaching class each day," Buggs said, certain that Ashley would turn him down.

"And he said, 'OK, you got it'—so I couldn't say no."

Buggs inherited a team full of girls who didn't play in the offseason, didn't work out regularly and weren't part of any travel ball teams. It was an exhausting challenge and one he wasn't looking forward to. "It certainly wasn't the plan to do it for the next sixteen years," he laughs. But that's what

Carl Buggs and his wife, Lakeisha, helped turn the Poly girls' program into a national power, winning six state titles (and counting) along the way. *Courtesy Thomas Cordova.*

happened; Buggs and Lakeisha have established one of the top programs in the nation, perennially ranked in the top ten in the country.

In Buggs's first season, the Jackrabbits lost the Moore League title to Wilson in the same year the Bruins went on to win a CIF title. The next year, the Jackrabbits went undefeated in Moore League play and made the CIF semifinals—from that point on, they took off like a rocket ship. Buggs's Poly teams played in a CIF championship game every year from 2002 to 2010 and as of 2015 have won six state titles and four CIF championships.

Players like Lillian Parker and Judith Smith helped bring Poly to the precipice in 2002, 2003 and 2004, but it finally got over the hump in '05 with Buggs's first CIF win over his old school, Lynwood. "At that time, they were a powerhouse, and we were trying to get there," Buggs says. "When I first got the job, I said, 'Let's scrimmage Lynwood, they're the best.' I told Ellis [Barfield, Lynwood's coach], 'Come at us like it's a CIF game.' It was probably 40–8 at halftime. I said, 'Alrighty, now we know where we're at.'"

The Jackrabbits went full circle in 2005, beating Lynwood 58–34 in the Pyramid, with a team starring Brittany Brumfield and a sensational freshman named Jasmine Dixon, who was named CIF Player of the Year. "Those kids had done a tremendous job, and Jas put us over the top," says Buggs. "From that point, it took off."

The Jackrabbits would make it to state and win a CIF state title each of the next four years, setting a new California record—an especially impressive feat given that Poly was playing in Division I against top competition.

Dixon continued to star and was named CIF Player of the Year all four years she was at Poly, earning Gatorade State Player of the Year honors and a McDonald's All-American nod as well before going on to Rutgers and then UCLA. The Jackrabbits were making the trip to Sacramento so regularly for the state title game that Lakeisha Buggs, who has been the top assistant for the team throughout her husband's entire tenure, could have opened up a travel agency.

Its opponent was the same the first three years—Berkeley High—and Poly beat Berkeley by an average of more than fifteen points. Dixon had plenty of help from talented players like April Cook and Candice Nichols, and her senior year saw one of the most talented teams in the history of California.

The 2008 Poly team, which went 31-2, was the consensus number two team in the nation. It featured Dixon (Rutgers, UCLA), Monique Oliver (Rutgers), Ashley and Brittany Wilson (Colorado), Ariya Crook Williams (USC), Kelli Thompson (UNLV), April Cook (Washington State) and Thaddesia Southall (USC, Long Beach State). In all, there were three All-

BASKETBALL IN LONG BEACH

All-American Jasmine Dixon, a star for the Jackrabbits in the mid-2000s. *Courtesy the* Press-Telegram's *Scott Varley.*

Americans on the team in Dixon, Oliver and Crook-Williams and eight NCAA Division I scholarship players.

"That was the best team we've ever had," says Buggs. "You look at that roster, and it was unheard of. There was a stretch there where we had like twenty kids playing Division I ball at the same time. We had kids West Coast, East Coast, everywhere. It was unbelievable."

It was almost as unbelievable that the Jackrabbits won their fourth-straight championship in 2009, not missing a beat with Dixon graduated. The addition of future LSU player Sheila Boykin helped tremendously, as Poly beat Monte Vista in Sacramento this time, by a score of 57–33. Kelli Thompson graduated and headed off to UNLV as the first player in state history to win four state championships in her career.

The next year, Poly won a CIF title, with Boykin earning CIF Player of the Year honors, but the Jackrabbits were stunned in state by an unheralded Oak Ridge team to halt their drive for five. A controversial call in the quarterfinals the next year broke Buggs's streak of nine straight CIF title appearances and cut short a promising season at 25-3, but Poly was back in the state championship in 2013, putting on a defensive clinic as it smothered its old rival, Berkeley, 46–28, with Kansas-bound Keyla Morgan starring and future Hawaii standout Destiny King.

To follow that up, in 2014, the Jackrabbits assembled probably the second most talented team in state history after their 2008 team.

Among the scholarship players were three-year starter and defensive fireplug Arica Carter (Louisville), McDonald's All-American Lajahna Drummer (UCLA), Jada Matthews (Utah), Justyce Dawson (Sacramento State), Emoni Jackson (Michigan) and Airica Carmon (Cal State Bakersfield). And that was just the senior class; the Jackrabbits also had future Pitt signee Tania Lamb and the nation's top freshman in USC-committed Ayanna Clark. They rolled to the first-ever CIF State Open Division crown, beating Salesian Prep 70–52.

The win moved Buggs into a tie with one other coach for most state titles in girls' basketball history, although Buggs says that doesn't motivate him. "I just take it a year at a time, and as long as my family is OK with it and I'm enjoying it, I'll keep coming back," he says. "I don't worry about that record; in fact, it was news to me when they told me I was tied. I just want to develop players and help them be successful. Championships come from that, but they're not what drives me."

Buggs is a strong coach who puts his players in a position to succeed and winds up collecting hardware on a yearly basis; in other words, he is the perfect model of a Long Beach Poly basketball coach.

BASKETBALL IN LONG BEACH

The Poly Way

There are many reasons for the school's success over the last 110 years—its coaches, for one, and a solid philosophy rooted in fundamentals and defense for another. The history has become its own driving force as well.

"They don't change coaches, they don't go out and get players and let them play how they want," says Burlison. "They still are the closest thing to the way things were. They have that continuity that other teams don't have. Programs now are good based on who they've hired. At Poly, you have players who are third- or fourth-generation Poly people, who could have gone to a lot of other schools but want to play where Dad and Granddad did."

The result is the rise and steady reign of the Jackrabbits, who have never gone more than twelve years without a CIF title in their lengthy history.

"Our school has been around since Jesus walked the earth, but we've always won," says Atkinson. "It's not like we were good eighty years ago and then fell off."

In its lengthy history, Poly has won more games, more playoff games and more CIF championships than any other school. And with a future based firmly in history, it's hard to imagine that reign ending.

6
Long Beach City College

The first big competition between rivals Long Beach Poly and Long Beach Wilson was not a sporting event at all. It was a simple inspection of both schools in April 1927. The winner's reward? Long Beach City College.

Since opening in 1927, Long Beach City College has earned a reputation for athletic success that rivals any junior college in the state of California, winning sixteen national titles and eighty-nine state championships. Of those eighty-nine state titles, seven have come on the hardwood, the most of any California junior college, led by some of the best coaches in Long Beach history in Lute Olson, Gary Anderson, Bill Fraser and Charlie Church while keeping some of the city's best talent in Long Beach for a couple more seasons.

Early Years

Long Beach City College opened on September 12, 1927 on the Long Beach Wilson campus, which was chosen over Poly thanks to the school being just one year old. The fledgling college opened with 503 students and 20 teachers.

One of those 20 teachers, Bert Smith, would kick off the athletic reputation of the city's first postgraduate school, along with Oak Smith and Clifford Wright, founders of the school's athletic program.

BASKETBALL IN LONG BEACH

The 1929 Vikings went undefeated in the conference and won the Southern California and state championships under coach Bert Smith—the first SoCal and state titles for LBCC. *Long Beach City College Foundation archive.*

A physical education teacher, Smith spent twenty-nine years with City College as a coach of numerous sports before retiring as the athletic director. He is also thought to have created the first junior college intramural sports program in the country.

Smith brought immediate success in basketball; the school's first team in the 1927–28 season took home a conference championship with an 8-2 record. But it was the 1929 team that earned the recognition of claiming the school's first state championship in any sport. It was also the first season a state title was offered in the California junior college ranks.

Dubbed the "Wonder Team of 1929," Bert's second team lost just one game all season, a 27–21 loss to the USC freshman squad over Christmas vacation. After a short preseason, the Vikings of 1929 rose from "veritable obscurity," as the yearbook described it, for a 10-0 conference mark.

Captained by John Frank, defensive ace Bill Davis and the fastest floor man in the Southland with "Peggy" Hopkins, Long Beach routed Glendale 44–7 in the conference opener before defeating Santa Ana 22–12. The Vikings downed Compton 40–12 in the next game to claim first place. Frank led the way with eighteen points in a 52–29 victory over Fullerton before crushing Pasadena by twenty-two points.

Long Beach was even more impressive in the second half of conference play, scoring 194 points in five games and holding its opponents to 77. The Vikings did get a fight from a physical Pasadena team in the regular-season finale before picking up a seven-point win.

After a perfect conference mark, San Bernardino stood in the Norsemen's way for a Southern California championship. The title would be decided in a best-of-three series.

San Bernardino gave Long Beach its closest game all season but a victory all the same as the Vikings came out ahead 32–25 in Game 1. The Norsemen broke the Indians after that, and Long Beach cruised to the title with a 54–22 victory in the second game.

Smith and the Vikings' wins put them up against Taft in the state championship game, a team described as the "classiest junior college team in the state" outside of Long Beach, as the yearbook pointed out.

In Game 1, Taft took a 13–8 lead in the first ten minutes, but a run from the trio of Davis, Frank and Hopkins gave the Southern California champs a 19–16 advantage at halftime. The defense found its form in the second half, holding Taft to just eight points for the 47–24 win on March 1. There was no looking back for Long Beach the next day; it grabbed a 22–8 halftime lead en route to a 45–20 win and the school's first state title. The school presented the "Long Beach Boys" with gold basketballs to commemorate the season.

Smith continued to bring success for one more season, guiding the program to an 11-1 record in 1930. The team's lone loss, a 32–26 defeat to Los Angeles, eliminated it from the conference championship race.

Smith's departure paved the way for Melvin Griffin. Oklahoma born and Kansas raised, Griffin coached multiple sports on campus, most notably baseball, where he won two Southern California championships.

Griffin had success his first couple seasons, striking gold with the 1932–33 team that brought back memories of the 1929 team. The Vikings won the Western Division championship and were crowned co-champions of Southern California with Fullerton. Led by Frank Schmidt, Kenny Purdy and Howell Crawford, the Norsemen went 6-0 in the conference, clinching the season with a 41–29 win over Santa Monica.

History will remember 1933 as the year a 6.4 magnitude earthquake rocked Long Beach on March 10, killing more than one hundred people. Long Beach was up 1-0 in the Southern California championship three-game series, having won the first game 40–38, when the earthquake hit.

BASKETBALL IN LONG BEACH

Head coach Melvin Griffin coaching the 1942 state champion squad. The 1942 team was the last to play before World War II suspended sports at City College for three years. *Long Beach City College Foundation archive.*

The earthquake postponed the second and third games, and due to the chaos of the first forty-eight hours, it became impossible to collect the teams. According to the City College yearbook, Fullerton refused to name new dates to play. The decision went to the commissioners of the league, who made the surprising move of naming the teams co-champions.

After two more conference titles, the 1941–42 season brought the program's second state title along with conference and Southern California championships.

The Vikings lost the conference opener by nine points to Compton, only to go on an eleven-game winning streak to finish 22-2. The Norsemen were led by city great and team captain Bob Howard, a six-foot-three guard and former Long Beach Poly star. Howard earned All-Conference and All-State honors on his way to Oregon State and eventually USC.

It was the last season before World War II suspended sports for three years. Griffin coached one more year after the hiatus, finishing his career with 185 wins and 82 losses, currently the fourth-winningest coach in program history.

BASKETBALL IN LONG BEACH

Charlie Church

An Idaho native, Charlie Church got his start at Long Beach Poly as the "B-level" coach before leading the varsity to three CIF titles after taking over in 1931. In 1942, Church left Poly for a stint in the Marine Corps, serving as a lieutenant colonel and coaching three service teams for a 90-2 record. He returned to Poly for a season before accepting the job at City College.

At the time, Herm Schwartzkopf, Long Beach State's first coach, was leading the program. Schwartzkopf was quite popular on campus—so much so that when rumors began spreading that he would not be retained as head coach after the 1948 season, students began circulating a petition to keep him.

One of Schwartzkopf's star players in his final season was Tom Amberry, who at the time was regarded as the program's greatest basketball player. Amberry would go on to set the Guinness World Record for consecutive free throws, with 2,750 in 1993 at the age of seventy-one (the record has since been broken).

Church was successful from the start, putting together a 26-10 season with a ten-game winning streak. After a 7-5 finish in the Metropolitan Conference in year two, Church and the program won three straight conference championships from 1951 through 1954. But after the three-peat, the Vikings finished in fourth place in 1955 before suffering two straight losing seasons that created grumblings from fans.

Church quickly silenced the unhappiness with some history. He brought Long Beach City College its third state title in 1957–58 with a 57–47 win over Oakland Junior College, which at the time had the best junior college defense ever, giving up 48.3 points per game.

The Vikings advanced to the title game despite five players contracting food poisoning, eking out a 70–57 win over rival Compton, pulling away in the final seven minutes.

In the championship game, Oakland jumped out to a 16–4 lead, but behind Bob Berry and Bill Jordan, the Vikings got within four at halftime.

Long Beach started poorly in the second half but used another late push, with Dick Markowitz putting Long Beach up 33–31 for its first lead. Markowitz and star rebounder Dave Jones made two big baskets down the stretch to hold off Oakland for the crown as the Vikings finished 27-4. But Church's next squad was even better.

After running through conference play, the defending champs entered the 1958–59 state tournament as the number two seed behind San Jose Junior College.

BASKETBALL IN LONG BEACH

Head coach Charlie Church and members of the 1958 state championship team on the cover of the *Saga* yearbook. Long Beach City College became the first school to win back-to-back state titles. *Long Beach City College Foundation archive.*

Long Beach quickly became the top seed after Ventura upset San Jose in the first round while the Vikings rallied from a ten-point deficit in the second half against Hancock.

That would be the closest contest for the Vikings in the tournament, as Long Beach rolled past Palomar 67–43 in the semifinals before defeating

BASKETBALL IN LONG BEACH

Santa Ana 75–67 in front of 3,700 fans at the Long Beach City College gym. Markowitz, MVP of the tournament, led the way with twenty-six points, despite fouling out in the third quarter.

City College became the first junior college to win two straight state titles, and with that milestone, Church rode off into the sunset. The coach left Long Beach with 235 wins, five conference titles, two state championships and another chapter in his legend.

LUTE OLSON

On September 27, 2002, longtime University of Arizona head coach Lute Olson officially became part of the Naismith Memorial Basketball Hall of Fame with a resume that included a national title with Arizona, 776 wins and five Final Fours.

But before Olson took his place among the basketball greats, he was just a high school coach in Southern California looking for a chance.

Born on a farm in Mayville, North Dakota, in 1934, Olson just seemed to have a knack for basketball. He led his high school team to a state title in 1952 before becoming a three-sport athlete at Augsburg College.

Olson immediately went into coaching after graduating in 1956, spending five years coaching prep basketball in Minnesota before moving to California in the early 1960s.

After several stops at local high schools in the Southland, Olson was fed up with the high school coaching scene.

"I decided I didn't want to be an old high school coach. The duties were ridiculous; we had restroom duties to make sure they were not smoking, lunch room duty," says Olson. "At the time, it was really demeaning."

Olson began talks with Moorpark Junior College and Saddleback College for assistant positions, but the departure of Rex Hughes for the University of Nebraska in 1969 left the City College job open. After Church left, City College went with Bob Hunt for five seasons and four from Chuck Kane, never reaching Church's success. Kane did, however, win two straight conference titles.

One of the top candidates was Jim Killingsworth, who had won a state title with Cerritos College in 1968, but Olson connected with athletic director Del Walker, quickly becoming Walker's favorite.

"Del indicated to the president that he wanted to hire me. He knew there was pressure by the administration to hire other candidates," says Olson. "Walker

BASKETBALL IN LONG BEACH

said, 'If you don't take Lute Olson as the basketball coach you better look for a new athletic director.'"

Walker's gamble paid off. Olson and the Vikings used the fast break to run all the way to the number two ranking in the state and the state finals for a match with number one Compton. Compton was undefeated and averaging more than one hundred points a game, the result being one of the greatest games in Long Beach history.

A crowd of four thousand packed the Long Beach gym to watch the two junior college giants do battle as Compton came out on top 77–75 in double overtime.

LBCC head coach Lute Olson later became the head coach of Long Beach State. Long Beach Press-Telegram *photo archive*.

"That was a tough loss for us. We were in position to win it, and we had done a really good job of controlling the ball for the last three minutes," says Olson. "It was really an exciting game. Compton was very talented. It was a great game."

"Greatest game of all time," says Gary Anderson, a freshman on that team, "so we shouldn't have lost."

The Vikings were on the wrong end of a controversial call—or lack of one. Jim Ferguson, who would go on to became the head coach at Wilson, found an open Anderson, who put up a five-foot bank shot for the win.

"I thought for sure I had made it," said Anderson. "But this guy, Michael Reed, went up through the basket and tipped it. It was goaltending, so for all intents and purposes, that should have been the end of the game."

BASKETBALL IN LONG BEACH

The 1970 LBCC Vikings lost the state championship 77–75 to Compton. *Long Beach City College Foundation archive.*

But nothing was called, and the game was sent to overtime. In an interview with the *San Bernardino Sun* years later, Anderson said he asked Reed about that shot.

"I ran into Reed and asked him if he goal tended my shot. He said, 'Sure, it was goaltending.'" said Anderson in the 2010 article. "I called Lute immediately and told him what Reed said. You never forget when you lose a game you should have won."

In the first overtime, Chuck Terry, the California Junior College Player of the Year, had a chance to put Long Beach up with three seconds left but missed the front end of a one-and-one to force double overtime.

"If I had a house," says Anderson, "I would have bet my house that he would make it."

With the game tied at 73–73 and under a minute left, Long Beach was called for an offensive foul. Compton's Ron Richardson put the Tartars up two for good with twenty-six seconds left.

BASKETBALL IN LONG BEACH

"I'll never forget when we lost," says Anderson. "[Lute] came to the chalkboard when the team was together. He got up there and said, 'We'll talk later because I'm too emotional to talk right now.'"

Olson and the Norsemen would have their redemption the next season when Long Beach brought home the program's fifth state title with a 57–54 victory over Cerritos.

Anderson had his own personal redemption, sealing the win with a pair of free throws with ten seconds left for a five-point lead.

Olson would end up leaving for Long Beach State after the 1973 season. He won 103 games in his four years—well on his way to an illustrious career.

Bill Fraser

While Olson's departure was certainly a disappointment, the program would be in good hands for the next thirty-seven years. After Hughes and Olson, Long Beach again hired a coach from the high school ranks in Wilson's Bill Fraser.

Questions were raised about Fraser's modest prep record of 143-98 and whether his quiet demeanor could be effective at the college level; one sportswriter referred to Fraser as "Mr. Personality" for his lack of emotion.

But the Canadian-born Fraser quickly silenced his critics, winning three straight conference titles in his first three seasons, including posting a 28-6 record in his first year and a trip to the state championship game before losing to Hancock 80–72.

After a semifinals loss in 1975, Fraser coached the Vikings back to the championship game in 1976, set to face Compton.

Things went well for the Vikings as they built a fourteen-point lead over their rival, but the Tartars rallied back. Long Beach tried to stall the ball, but three turnovers allowed Compton to make it a 63–62 Vikings lead with nineteen seconds to go. The game was placed in the hands of Dean Decker, Fraser's former All-CIF player at Wilson. Decker was fouled on the inbounds and calmly sank two free throws to ice the game for the program's second title of the decade and sixth overall.

Fraser's career at City College would stretch seventeen years as the man who some thought was too calm for the job surpassed Church as the school's all-time win leader, with 374 wins. He retired in 1990 with 517 wins combined with Long Beach and Wilson.

Fraser, who passed away in 2014, averaged twenty-three wins per season and won five conference titles, leading the Vikings to the postseason thirteen times with six trips to the Final Four.

Gary Anderson

The program's next coach, Gary Anderson, seemed destined to lead the Vikings after playing for Olson and serving as an assistant to Fraser since 1975.

Like his predecessors Olson and Fraser, Anderson, a Poly graduate, led his first team to the state championship. Forward Terry Nelson, who would go on to Cincinnati, powered the Vikings on the court, but Long Beach fell 73–70 to Rancho Santiago in the title match. Nelson cut the lead to two points with seven seconds to go while the defense forced a jump ball to regain possession with two seconds remaining. Sheldon Grigsby's last-second shot hit the back of the rim.

The Vikings returned to the title game in 1994, led by Kevin Beal, Marcus Rodgers, Mark Neal and Sharrief Metoyer, who went on to win two CIF titles as the head coach at Poly.

Long Beach faced Chaffey in the semifinals, coached by first-year head coach George Tarkanian, whose legendary father, Jerry, was an assistant coach. Anderson watched Chaffey, who deployed the elder Tarkanian's famous Amoeba zone defense, crush San Jose City by fifty points.

Anderson devised an offensive game plan around a 1-4 set mixed in with a triangle offense to find the space against the legendary defense, running screens for Beal to the inside and screens for Rodgers. The Vikings ended up winning by twenty points.

"After the game, Jerry, whom I had been friends with, came up and said that was the best anyone has attacked that amoeba," said Anderson. "I think that was the best compliment I ever had."

The win set up a date with the number one ranked Ventura. The two programs put on a classic championship tilt with thirty-six lead changes by Anderson's memory. Beal scored nineteen points followed by seventeen for Rogers, but it was a layup by Metoyer with 1:44 left that put Long Beach up as it held on for a 63–61 win and the program's seventh state championship.

Afterward, college coaches in the stands came up to Anderson to tell him that that was one of the best junior college games they had ever seen.

BASKETBALL IN LONG BEACH

That 1994 win marks the last state championship for Long Beach, still the most in California junior college history. Anderson spent eighteen years as head coach, with a one-year break, surpassing Fraser as the school's all-time winningest coach, with 378 wins and seven conference championships. He still serves as an assistant to the program after retiring as head coach in 2009.

LBCC WOMEN

The pioneer for women's sports at Long Beach City College was a Pennsylvania native by the name of Elizabeth "Betty" Crilley. Born in Oil City, Pennsylvania, Crilley moved to Pasadena to attend college, earning degrees from USC and the University of Illinois before getting hired by City College in 1955.

Before Crilley, women participated in sports among themselves on campus, but her arrival marked a step forward for women's athletics.

Crilley coached for twenty years, coaching every sport en route to fifteen league titles and six all–junior college championships until 1975, when she became the school's first athletic director for women's sports.

The advent of Title IX was the catalyst for colleges and high schools developing varsity sports for women, as well as chances for women coaches.

Donna Prindle was one of those young coaches. A former basketball and volleyball star at Long Beach State, Prindle was hired as a part-time coach for basketball and softball in 1976.

While Title IX provided a big boost, Prindle's early squads faced numerous challenges. They had no scoreboard (a student would write the score on a chalkboard), and they also lacked a clock, borrowing a field clock from the football team. Prindle would also serve as the team's bus driver for away games. Sometimes the team rented separate cars to make it to games, and on at least one occasion, the team got split up on the drive. Prindle quickly learned to put the starting five in her car so they could at least start the game despite missing players.

But despite the limitations, Prindle and her talented players found success. Toni Bell-Skeen was the first woman in Long Beach City College history to earn an athletic scholarship, averaging twenty-four points and ten rebounds in 1976. Kari Jondle-Burke helped Long Beach to back-to-back conference titles in 1982 and 1983 and was named conference MVP after setting the school record for points in a season. Prindle, a member of the California

BASKETBALL IN LONG BEACH

Community College Athletic Association Hall of Fame, led Long Beach to seven conference titles in her career and a runner-up finish in the state playoffs in 1988—her final season coaching basketball.

Prindle's name is prominent in not just athletic history but also Long Beach history for her lawsuit in the early 1980s that affected the junior college landscape.

In 1982, City College underwent budget cuts, leading to the removal of Crilley and her position. The loss of Crilley was a wakeup call to female coaches and athletes, leading to a series of inquires that in turn led to the discovery that City College was in violation of Title IX, funding men's programs while cutting women's programs.

Prindle, along with Peggy Stoll, the gymnastics coach, reached out to the ACLU to have their case taken up. It was picked up by renowned lawyer Daniella Sapriel, who was well known for arguing in front of the Supreme Court for women's right to compete in the distance events in the 1984 Olympics.

The case was filed in 1984 and took five years to reach the courtroom. At the downtown LA Supreme Court on the day of the trial, Sapriel was anxious and nervous. Prindle had to calm down the star lawyer like she was her star player before a big game.

"She told me, 'I wanna win this more than anything I've ever done in court,'" says Prindle.

City College sent no one to the courthouse besides its lawyer, prompting the judge to hold a conference in chambers, where Long Beach's counsel was advised to settle for fear of wasting the court's time.

Long Beach City College settled in 1989, and the entire department underwent changes as junior college administrations all over the state followed the *Prindle v. Long Beach City College* case and used it as an example.

Today, Prindle, a member of the City College Hall of Champions, teaches in the Physical Education Department at Cerritos College. The Vikings women's program has again begun to flourish, this time under the direction of Mike Anderson, who has had LBCC ranked among California's best for the last few seasons.

7
Long Beach Wilson

As the second-oldest high school in Long Beach, Wilson High has a basketball tradition dating back more than eighty years. It's true the Bruins do not have the championship history of their Moore League counterparts, but that has not stopped Wilson alumni and coaches from contributing to the city's rich basketball success.

Early Years

Wilson opened its doors in 1926, dedicated on January 28, 1927, the first year the Bruins would put forth a basketball team. The inaugural squad was led by head coach Fred Frazer, dubbed the "Battling Bears."

The Bruins lost the program's first game, an 18–9 decision to Compton and finished the season at 4-3, winning the final three games.

Year two featured a school record nine straight wins behind captain Mike Sagerhorn, but the Bruins ended up falling to Santa Monica in the league championship game.

In 1930, Frazer led the program to its first league championship in the Bay League, but the next season trumped even that historic run.

Led by "Droopy" Masterson, Wilson finished 19-1, their lone loss to Whittier in the Southern California championship game, now known as the California Interscholastic Federation (CIF). Wilson cruised through most

BASKETBALL IN LONG BEACH

A team photo of the 1931 Wilson Bruins, arguably the greatest team in school history, losing in the Southern California championship game by three points. *Long Beach Wilson yearbook archive.*

of the Bay League, winning narrow victories over Compton (29–20) and Glendale (20–15) with capacity crowds watching in the East End Gym.

A 41–19 win over Pasadena forced a tie for first place with rival Long Beach Poly. The teams met at nearby Huntington Park gym during the "suffocating" heat of March, as the yearbook described. Behind the play of Frank Schmidt, known as the "Teuton Terror," Wilson prevailed 28–16 for the Bay League title, and fans began calling this the greatest victory in Wilson history.

In the playoffs, Wilson knocked off the defending Southern League champs, Coronado, 25–20 before staging a comeback against Chino at Whittier College for a 26–21 victory to set up a date for the Southland title with powerhouse Whittier, which had won the first three Southern California championships in CIF history. Wilson, without star Schmidt, who was ailing with the flu, fell 25–22—still the lone CIF title game the program has reached.

The remainder of the 1930s was not kind to Wilson. The next two seasons, the Bruins combined for just four wins. In 1936 and 1937, Wilson won one game each year. In 1933, the Bruins lost by one point to Inglewood after a timer error resulted in six extra minutes being played. Part of the woes came from the fact that the Bruins did not have a gym in which to practice on campus. The team was forced to walk two and a half miles to the Armory.

BASKETBALL IN LONG BEACH

The early 1940s brought back some of the glory days that the Bruins had enjoyed under Frazer. In 1940, the team won its first league title since 1931, sharing the Foothill League crown with Whittier and Glendale. While the Bruins were able to sweep Whittier, they lost out on sole possession with a one-point loss to Alhambra and a six-point loss to Glendale. That team was led by a bright star in Horace "Al" Brightman, one of the best players and coaches Long Beach has ever produced.

Horace "Al" Brightman

Horace Brightman was born on September 22, 1923, in Eureka, California, and quickly became one of the best athletes in Long Beach. After leading the Bruins to a league title in 1940, Brightman led the Bruins again in 1941 but couldn't quite replicate the team's success. Wilson finished second in the Foothill League and City League. Brightman enjoyed a sensational senior season, averaging a city-high 22.7 points per game, including a fifty-one-point performance against Leuzinger. The senior was placed on the All-State team, as well as earning CIF Player of the Year honors.

Brightman was drafted by the Cleveland Indians out of Wilson and played minor-league ball in 1942 with the Springfield Rifles and Baltimore Orioles before being drafted again, this time by the navy. Once out of the service, Brightman earned a roster spot with a brand-new franchise in the Basketball Association of America, which would become the NBA in 1949: the Boston Celtics. Brightman was a starter for the 1946–47 season, becoming the first Wilson player to play professional basketball. The former Bruin played fifty-eight games with the Celtics, averaging 9.8 points per game, and held the single-game franchise record for Boston, with 26 points in a December game against the Chicago Stags.

So why just one season with the Celtics? In a story chronicled by Seattle native and Northwest sports historian David Eskenazi, in the offseason, Brightman drove to Seattle to visit family with his wife, Katie. He told the *Seattle Times* that he left his wallet in an Idaho motel, and when the couple returned to retrieve it, they kept driving west.

While looking for work, Brightman joined the Pacific Coast Professional Basketball League as a player/coach for the Seattle Athletics for one year (1947–48). That season got the attention of Seattle University, and at the age of twenty-four, Brightman was hired as the head coach in August

BASKETBALL IN LONG BEACH

1948. He would be integral in the rise of the two-year-old program to a regional power.

Brightman's first two teams went a combined 24-31, but from then on, it was consistent dominance for the next five seasons. In 1951, the team finished 32-5, followed by an NIT appearance in 1952 with a 27-8 record.

Brightman's 1952 squad will go down as one of the most memorable in college basketball history, the team that upset Abe Saperstein's Harlem Globetrotters 84–81 in the Edmundson Pavilion before 12,500 fans. The game was part of a fundraising tour for the nation's Olympic efforts, but after the loss, Saperstein promptly cancelled the rest of tour, according to the *Seattle Post-Intelligencer*.

Five-foot-nine Johnny O'Brien, Brightman's star player along with his twin brother, Eddie, led the nation in scoring with twenty-seven points per game, and that January night he shined with forty-three points. As the twins remember, it was Saperstein's mouth that doomed his Globetrotters.

"Before the game, we were under the north stands, and the Globetrotters were on the other side," Johnny O'Brien told the *Seattle Post-Intelligencer* in 2002. "Saperstein came over, looked at us and said, 'Is this all you got?' That's where we won the ballgame."

The win catapulted Seattle onto the national stage. The 1953 season began four straight NCAA Tournament appearances, and Brightman led the Chieftains to the Sweet Sixteen three times. But in an interesting turn of events, Brightman resigned after the 1956 season; many in the Seattle area pointed to Brightman's final game, a twenty-four-point loss to John Wooden and UCLA, as the reason for his departure.

Reports of that NCAA game describe it as one of the roughest in its day, a game that saw two near fights, three UCLA starters foul out and sixty combined fouls—thirty-five on the Bruins, then the NCAA record. According to historian Eskenazi, citing the *Seattle Post-Intelligencer*, after the intense game, Brightman tried to pick a fight with Wooden.

Brightman would resign three days later, telling media there was no pressure to resign but that it had been planned for a while. Still, the speculation in Seattle was that administrators at the Jesuit institute did not care for Brightman's supposed post-game antics.

The timing was also puzzling considering Brightman was on the verge of gaining a player who would go down as one of the greatest to ever play the game in Elgin Baylor. Brightman was paramount in getting Baylor, a future number one draft pick for the Lakers and a Naismith Memorial Basketball Hall of Fame member, to Seattle from the College of Idaho. Baylor eventually led the Chieftains to the national title game in 1958 before they fell to Kentucky.

BASKETBALL IN LONG BEACH

Wilson great Al Brightman, coach of Seattle University, shaking hands with John Wooden in 1956. *Long Beach Press-Telegram photo archive.*

After leaving, Brightman returned to Long Beach and got his degree at Long Beach State, bouncing around odd jobs before landing coaching jobs in the American Basketball League (ABL) and American Basketball Association (ABA), including for the Long Beach Chiefs in 1962.

Brightman, inducted into the Long Beach Century Club and Wilson Halls of Fame, eventually moved back to the Northwest—to Portland—until his death in 1992.

Start of the Moore League

After becoming the first basketball coach in school history in 1927, Frazer retired after the 1945–46 season. Bob Hunt became the second coach in Wilson basketball history but stayed just three seasons. Hunt did have a local

BASKETBALL IN LONG BEACH

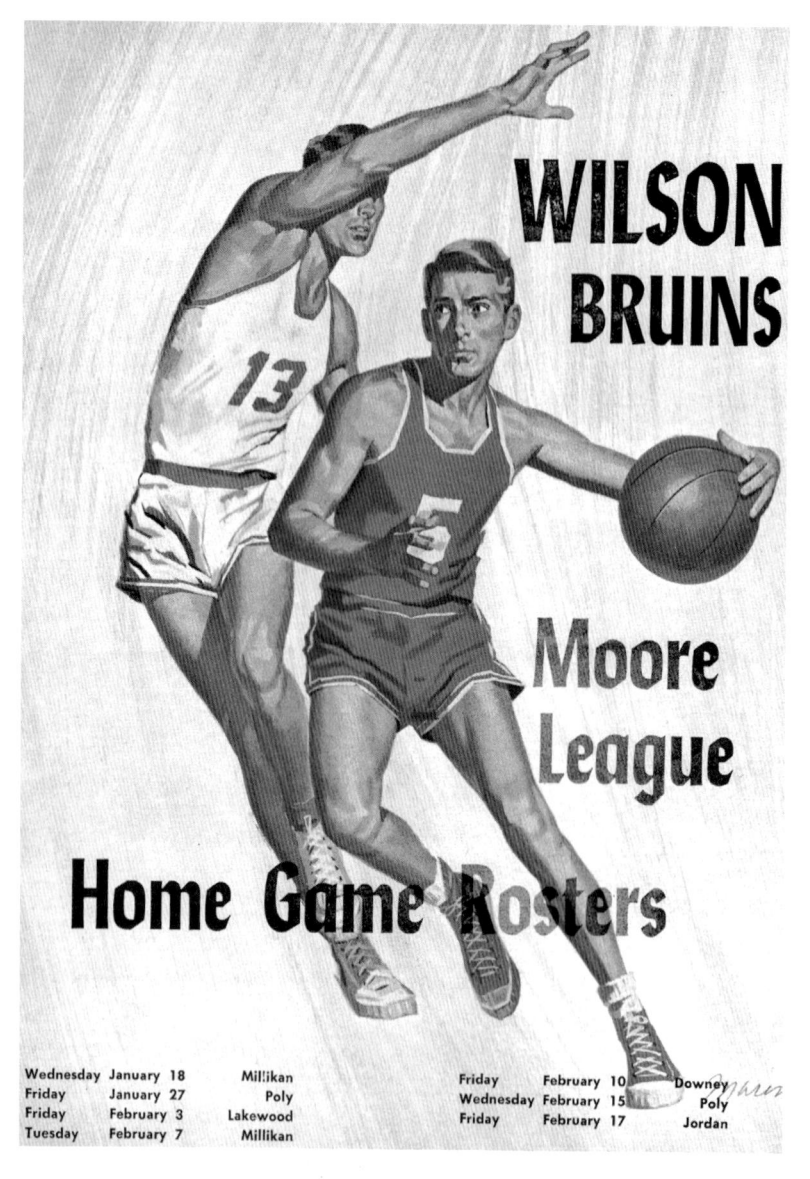

Wednesday January 18	Millikan	
Friday January 27	Poly	
Friday February 3	Lakewood	
Tuesday February 7	Millikan	
Friday February 10	Downey	
Wednesday February 15	Poly	
Friday February 17	Jordan	

Wilson basketball's Moore League schedule program. *Long Beach Wilson yearbook archive.*

star in Richard Perry, who would go on to become head coach of Long Beach State basketball in the 1960s. Bob Howard took over in 1950 but lasted just one season, paving the way for Bill Patterson in '51. Patterson's first season coincided with the new Wilson gym, the first time the Bruins had a true home court in seventeen years.

BASKETBALL IN LONG BEACH

The new coach immediately made the Bruins competitive with powers Compton and Poly. Wilson knocked off defending CIF champion Compton in Patterson's first season, and the Jackrabbits needed overtime to escape with a win.

In 1953–54, Patterson finally put together a championship team, sharing the Coast League with Poly. The Bruins ripped off an eleven-game winning streak, defeating the Jackrabbits 60–58 along the way. However, it was Poly that ended that streak with a 52–50 victory, but an eleven-point win over Jordan earned Wilson a share of the crown.

The future was bright for Wilson after the "B team" won twenty-seven games with a 12-0 league mark. But Patterson was gone soon after that season, eventually ending up at Long Beach State like Perry.

Bob Robbins faced the task of following Patterson and also leading Wilson into the new Moore League era in the 1957–58 season. Robbins put together back-to-back runner-up seasons behind Poly, the closest he would come to leading the Bruins to a Moore League title.

The coach who followed would be the man to finally do it.

Bill Fraser

Saying the name Bill Fraser in local basketball circles will invoke the memory of one of the city's best coaches. But back in 1958, Fraser was just a junior varsity basketball and track coach at Wilson. Fraser got the head-coaching gig for the Bruins after Robbins left in 1965 and was off to a fast start with a 19-7 record and a second-place finish. Tied with Millikan, Wilson lost a post-league playoff game with the Rams by one point and was left out of the playoffs.

It wasn't until 1971 that history was finally made. Fraser and the Bruins posted a 22-7 record, a 9-1 mark in the Moore League. Wilson lost the league opener to Millikan but ripped off nine straight wins for the first Moore League crown in school history. John Sagehorn was named the league's Player of the Year.

The good times kept rolling as Wilson pulled off its second league crown in 1973 after being projected to finish third. The call up of Dean Decker, a future star at Long Beach City College, from junior varsity proved to be the difference; Wilson went 9-1 in the league again, pulling out three wins by a combined seven points. The Bruins locked up the title with a triple-overtime victory over Compton.

BASKETBALL IN LONG BEACH

Fraser ended his Wilson tenure on a high note, with 143 wins, 98 losses and the program's only Moore League titles, leaving for the position at City College where he would win a state title and cement his status as one of the city's best coaches.

Wilson could have had a couple more Moore League titles on the banner considering a future ABA Rookie of the Year was walking on campus. Swen Nater, hailing from the Netherlands, is the best Bruin who never played for Wilson. Nater moved to Long Beach when he was nine, not speaking a word of English. In high school, he stood six-foot-eight and loved basketball but was cut from the team his junior year and apparently told not to return.

Head coach Bill Fraser, one of Long Beach's all-time winningest coaches, instructing his Bruins during the 1973 Moore League championship season. *Long Beach Wilson yearbook archive.*

"I think it was my physical education teacher who said he'd never seen anything work that hard and move that slow," Nater told the *New York Times* in a 2004 profile. "I couldn't jump, but I had a good set of hands and I could shoot. But nobody saw that or wanted to develop that, even though I was the tallest kid."

Nater grew to six-foot-eleven and made the team at Cypress College, blossoming into a junior college All-American. He eventually earned a scholarship from Wooden and UCLA, winning two national titles backing up the great Bill Walton. Nater enjoyed an eleven-year career in the ABA and NBA, winning the 1974 Rookie of the Year Award in the ABA. He is the only player to lead both leagues in rebounding.

Wilson is still searching for that next Moore League crown since Fraser but has produced several standout players and teams.

Under former Long Beach City College star Jim Ferguson, regarded as one of the city's best coaches during his tenure, the Bruins upset the number

BASKETBALL IN LONG BEACH

one nationally ranked Poly and produced Moore League Player of the Year Don Brotz.

Wilson has had a couple of other top players walk its halls in Mike Wilder (UC Irvine), another Moore League Player of the Year, and future NBA player Michael Batista, who played for the Memphis Grizzlies and won three Euroleague championships.

Paula Clear

Wilson fielded its first girls' team in 1977 under head coach Margaret Kemp, and as expected, the Lady Bruins struggled on the varsity level. It wasn't until the hire of Long Beach State great Margaret Mohr that they turned the corner.

Mohr played for the 49ers under legendary head coach Joan Bonvicini, leading Long Beach to the 1987 Final Four. Mohr served as an assistant at Long Beach State and Santa Clara before landing at Wilson in the 1990s. She brought the first Moore League title to the program in 1997 and another in 1998, with Wilson advancing all the way to the CIF Southern Section 1-AA championship game. Yet the Bruins' magic ran out in the title game, when they fell 55–40 to Peninsula. Mohr took the position at Cypress College after that, leading the Chargers to a state championship in 2005. Luckily for the Bruins, their next coach was already living in Long Beach.

Paula Clear played at UNLV with coaching stints with Whittier and Montebello before applying for the Wilson job. Clear picked up where Mohr left off, and Wilson won its third straight Moore League crown in 1999.

Clear had a distinct vision for her team entering the 2000 season: make it to the Walter Pyramid, the location of the CIF championship game. She made motivational posters for her team, depicting the stairs of the Pyramid.

The Bruins won their fourth-straight Moore League title, losing just once to Lakewood, a loss that Clear called pivotal in giving her team a reality check.

Despite being led by Rutgers-bound Dawn McCulloch, Wilson was an unheralded team entering the playoffs.

"We weren't seeded in the top four or six in the bracket," remembers Clear. "We were pretty much the underdog."

The Southern Section knew the Bruins were for real when Wilson upset the number one seed Ayala in the semifinals to reach its second CIF title game in three years. Wilson would face number two seed Lynwood, making its fifth CIF championship game since 1990.

Early on, the Knights showed why they were one of the top programs in the nation, dominating the Bruins for the majority of the match, building a fourteen-point lead with 5:30 left on the clock. But unwilling to leave empty-handed again, McCulloch and Wilson mounted a furious rally, turning on the pressure defense.

"It was a whirlwind…we forced turnovers. Our kids were all over the floor. Dawn made some clutch shots. It was fun," says Clear. "I remember feeling like it was in slow motion when we were coming back, like this is a dream."

The defense held the Knights scoreless for the remainder of the game as the senior McCulloch poured in nine of her twenty-three points in that run, her free throws with 1:20 left putting Wilson up for good.

Lynwood had a desperation heave at the basket, and the ball bounced off the rim before Wilson could celebrate the school's first CIF basketball title.

Clear won one more league championship in 2005 before retiring several years later—the last Moore League title for Wilson basketball.

8
LONG BEACH JORDAN

Jordan athletic director Lamarr Biffle gave a sobering pronouncement about the Panthers' history not too long ago. "This school has kind of always been known for underachieving," he said.

For much of Jordan's past, it's hard to argue with him. Jordan had two of the greatest players in Long Beach history with Larry Hudson and James Hardy in the 1970s, but neither would ever get to play in a playoff game, as the Panthers couldn't quite break into the Moore League's top three to grab a postseason berth.

The school was founded in 1933, right after the earthquake that leveled most of the city's schools. Between that disaster and the Depression, the money that had been planned to build Jordan ended up elsewhere, and North Long Beach's high school started out with classes being held at the Long Beach YMCA for two years before the first buildings were constructed.

The Panthers' basketball team had early success against Wilson but couldn't manage to beat its rivals down Atlantic Avenue, Long Beach Poly. Finally, in 1943, after ten years, it beat Wilson and Poly to claim the All-City Championship, with Jack Schlecht earning All-City and All-CIF honors. Jordan competed in the Sunset League in those days, along with Orange, Santa Ana, Huntington Beach and other Orange County schools.

In 1950, the Panthers—who nicknamed their lower-level teams the "Kitty Cats"—opened a new gym under head coach Ben Palmgren, hosting LA Jordan in the facility's first contest on October 28, 1950. The team slowly built itself up throughout the '50s, with stars such as Tom Batson and Ron

BASKETBALL IN LONG BEACH

Larry Hudson was a star for the Panthers in the early 1970s. *Press-Telegram file photo.*

Fairly. Fairly was a multi-sport star at Jordan and would go on to a twenty-one-year career in Major League Baseball, including a twelve-year stint with the Dodgers, winning three World Series.

But before Fairly decided to play baseball for Rod Dedeaux at USC, he was actually offered a basketball scholarship by John Wooden at UCLA after a senior year that saw him average eighteen points per game.

Palmgren would lead the Panthers to the Moore League title in 1958, just the second year that the all-Long Beach league was in existence. The Panthers were upset in the first round of CIF that year, however, and they wouldn't win another league title until 1963, when Palmgren's Panthers went 8-2 in the league and clinched the title in an overtime win against Poly. Jim DeLong was named All-CIF that year for a twenty-six-point-per-game campaign.

After the 1965 season, Palmgren gave way to coach Bob Cook, who would coach great players like Chuck Terry, Larry Hudson and James Hardy.

Terry graduated in 1968 with All-State honors and was named the California Junior College Player of the Year while at LBCC; he then went on to play for Long Beach State before being selected in the NBA draft by the Milwaukee Bucks. Hudson was a local star who made a huge splash in signing with Long Beach State over several other suitors after a prep career that saw him named All-State twice and All-American his senior year. James Hardy opted for the University of San Francisco and would enjoy a twelve-year pro career, including four years with the Jazz. "He was arguably the best basketball talent to ever come out of Long Beach from then until today," says local hoops guru Frank Burlison. "He was so physically dominating."

Cook was great at developing players, but his Panthers teams weren't getting over the hump. In his last year, they went 1-19, and the Jordan administration made the decision to hire Ron Massey away from Long Beach Poly, where he'd been running the JV program for three years.

Ron Massey

No coach or player is more synonymous with any school—perhaps in any sport—in Long Beach than Ron Massey is with Jordan. Massey's name is never brought up without someone talking about his great Panthers teams, and rarely do North Long Beach sports come up in conversation without someone mentioning Massey.

"What a great human being, a stoic guy," says Long Beach hoops guru Frank Burlison. "He never talked unless he had something of significance to say—he had as much impact on the players he coached and taught as any coach in Long Beach history."

The first game Massey coached in late 1982 saw his Panthers lose by more than forty points to St. Bernard. Massey laminated Burlison's *Press-Telegram* article from that game and pulled it out of his bag after he coached his last game in 2010. "They came so far," says Burlison.

It didn't happen overnight. Massey's first season saw Jordan finish 5-20, and the team didn't win a single Moore League game his second year. But his

BASKETBALL IN LONG BEACH

ability to develop players and build a cohesive team around old-school discipline caught on quickly, and in 1985, Jordan was in the postseason for the first time in twenty years.

"I can truly say that each year the program has become a little better," he said at the time. "We've only just turned the corner as far as turning the program around—next year we're looking for even more improvement."

Three years later, Jordan was ranked in the CIF, and then, in 1990–91, the breakthrough finally happened. Massey coached a team with all five starters returning. The season began with high expectations, as one of the Panthers' star players that year, Joel Rosborough, recalls.

"It's kind of weird, but we expected to go that far. Jordan never won a championship before, but we expected it," he says. "We never talked about it, and Massey wouldn't let us talk about it, but that's what we expected."

Ron Massey changed everything about Jordan when he arrived on campus; he's seen here in his second year as coach, in 1983. *Jordan yearbook.*

With Rodney Harris, Darryl Bryant, Deandre Smith and Rosborough leading the way, the Panthers stormed to a Moore League title—the first at Jordan since 1963. Then they ran the table in the playoffs, which were dominated by superior Moore League teams. The Panthers beat Lakewood in the semifinals, 78–66, and then advanced to the championship, where they faced off against a Millikan team led by Pat Thacker and Dante Powell.

BASKETBALL IN LONG BEACH

Jordan prevailed again, winning the 1-AA championship 69–67 at the LA Sports Arena. "The kids proved what you can achieve if you work hard enough," Massey said.

"North Long Beach got the most out of it," remembers Rosborough. "It was the biggest thing in our part of town for at least a couple of weeks." North Town partied for a solid seven nights after the championship, as up-and-coming rapper DJ Quick went from house party to house party putting on shows. "It was amazing," says Rosborough.

Massey's Panthers would win another pair of CIF championships in 1993 and 1996. In '93, Jordan prevailed against Simi Valley 61–59 in double overtime, thanks to Everett Ratleff's twenty-nine points, including a buzzer-beating game-winner that sent him off to Long Beach State on a high note. In '96, Jordan went 30-4 and won the title 54–38 over Victor Valley. Ortege Jenkins played on both teams before going on to star as a quarterback at Arizona.

Jordan hasn't won a CIF championship since, although Massey did coach several more league champion teams (he coached seven of the nine league champs in school history). It also produced one of the best hoopers to come out of Long Beach in the last half century in Travon Bryant, who was at Jordan in the late '90s. The six-foot-nine Bryant was a star in high school, playing in the McDonald's All-American Game and being named to the PARADE All-American team before heading to Missouri for college ball. Since then, he's had a twelve-year career

Travon Bryant in his senior season, arguably the finest basketball player to ever come out of Jordan. *Jordan yearbook.*

playing overseas for a number of teams, most recently the Akita Northern Happinets in Japan.

Finally, after three decades, three CIF championships, seven league titles and over five hundred wins, Massey retired in 2010. "When he won, he made Jordan basketball relevant," says Burlison. "They were never going to equal Poly, but they were close enough to make it a legitimate rivalry."

Rosborough was one of several Panthers alums who came back to coach with Massey (including James Corbett) and would end up succeeding him in 2010, after ten years of serving as his top assistant. "He was the most consistent coach, almost to a fault," says Rosborough. "He ran the exact same plays for twenty years—never changed plays or defenses and never called them anything different."

Massey Passes

On January 10, 2014, Jordan officially renamed the court at the school Ron Massey Court. Many other gyms in Long Beach are named after their best coaches, but Jordan chose to honor Massey's wishes in specifically renaming the hard court.

Jordan principal Shawn Ashley said Massey was specific about how he wanted to be recognized. "Ron made it clear he wanted the floor named after him," he said at the time.

The reason?

"When I first got to Jordan," Massey remembered, "the court was the main thing to me. Taking care of that basketball court was so important. I used to sweep it down, dust it before practice and before every game. I worked on it every day."

It was a hard task during storms. "We had holes in the ceiling," Massey said, "and it would rain on the floor. We needed mops and buckets before the games; we'd sometimes have to towel it off during breaks in the game. That court became like my kitchen floor. It was part of my house."

It was a packed house for the dedication, which came at halftime during a game against Poly. Massey was emotional in thanking the crowd with his deep, booming voice. "Thank you for giving me my flowers while I'm still around to smell them," he said. After the ceremony, he elaborated, "For this to happen while I'm still alive to enjoy it…It's going to hit me on that day when I can sit up there and see my name on the floor. That'll be worth a million dollars to me."

BASKETBALL IN LONG BEACH

As it turned out, the great coach's words were somewhat prophetic. Shockingly, Massey passed away just three months later, at the age of sixty-five, only a few years into his retirement with his wife, Shirley.

It's a loss the North Long Beach community is still reeling from.

"He represents what the community is all about," said his fellow coach and friend Ron Palmer, who coached at Poly against Massey. "He's forever a part of the legacy that Long Beach has with its players and athletes and coaches. He established a tremendous tradition at Jordan, where there hadn't been one—he's just one of those Long Beach legends."

The CIF Hall of Fame coach's legacy still looms large over the part of town to which he dedicated his life.

"When you say Jordan, he's the image," says Rosborough. "He never lived in North Long Beach, but he took the job, and he devoted himself. He wanted to put it on the map. Basketball was a small part of it—the way he did it is the thing that people appreciate the most. As a PE teacher, he touched lives that don't get into the paper, the girls who needed counseling, the knuckleheads. Everyone loved him, or if you didn't, you respected him."

Under Massey, Jordan was an underachiever no more but rather a big-time player on the Southern California basketball scene.

Panther Girls

Jordan's girls' teams never hit the heights that Massey's boys' teams did; the Lady Panthers have won just two Moore League titles. Lorie Lindahl coached the team for more than two decades, winning a league crown in 1977. Lindahl was a star at both of Long Beach's colleges and is in the Hall of Fame at LBCC and

Lorie Lindahl was the coach of the Panthers' girls' team for twenty-five years and is a famous basketballer in town, as well as a member of the Long Beach State and LBCC Halls of Fame. *Jordan yearbook.*

BASKETBALL IN LONG BEACH

Long Beach State. She led the Panthers to the CIF quarterfinals in 1982, the furthest in team history. The second league title was claimed by head coach Lisa Ulmer's team in 1996, when the Panthers were led by Antoinette Bryant and Reta Sula.

9
ST. ANTHONY

Long Beach has always been known for its big public high schools, with Poly, Wilson and others churning out top-level professional and Olympic athletes. But since 1920, there's been a small private powerhouse chugging along downtown as well, just a stone's throw from the Jackrabbits' home. That school is St. Anthony, Long Beach's only Catholic high school and home to some fascinating hoops history as well.

A Historic Tournament

Toward the tail end of World War II, in early 1945, the St. Anthony student body pitched in volunteer hours to put on the Southern California Catholic Girls' Basketball Tournament. The Saints, playing in skirts and overcoats, won the inaugural event, but nobody gathered there could have predicted the history that would unroll for the tournament.

It would end up as Southern California's longest-running basketball tournament for either sex, being held annually from that first year until the 2010–11 season—an incredible run of sixty-six years.

The Saints were often the victors; they won the first five tournament champions. Very quickly, the event laid the foundation for what we now think of as a modern tournament. By the late '40s, it was a sold-out event

BASKETBALL IN LONG BEACH

Crowd shots from the late 1940s at the St. Anthony Girls' Basketball Tournament—one of the longest-running girls' tourneys in California. *St. Anthony yearbook.*

with the winning team taking home a trophy and the All-Tournament team members each getting a plaque.

The event, which was usually filled with smaller Catholic schools like St. Anthony, became such a big annual event that rivalries contained entirely within the tournament began to develop. St. Anthony and St. Mary's met on an almost yearly basis for the tournament championship during the 1950s.

Because girls' basketball didn't have a full varsity season until Title IX's passage in the 1970s, the tournament took on a larger significance for the St. Anthony program. It was, in effect, the entire preseason, league schedule and postseason boiled down into one event, which saw fans come from all over Southern California, as well as big performances by the Saints' student body.

Sadly, the event came to an end (at least temporarily) in 2010–11, ironically because the Saints were too successful. It was the season after they'd won the CIF championship and had an All-American on the roster.

"It was always a small Catholic schools tournament, and they didn't want to play us that year," remembers Saints athletic director Brian Walsh. "We tried inviting the bigger schools, but they were already locked into the big sponsored tournaments at Mater Dei or in Arizona."

There has been talk of reviving the tournament, but regardless of whether that happens, it still has a special place in California basketball history. "I know when I was a student, we would always volunteer to run it," recalls Walsh, who graduated in 1995. "When I came back as an AD, I started researching it, and I was amazed at the history. My mom said it was a really big deal when she was a student back in the 1960s. It's just really special. There was no press coverage, no recognized champions for girls' basketball back then, so to have this tournament with all this history is really meaningful."

Bill Bond

Of course, the St. Anthony boys made plenty of history, too. In the early 1950s, the Saints had the state's Mr. Basketball in Bill Bond, who was named CIF Player of the Year in 1953. Bond dropped fifty-nine points on Serra his senior season to set a CIF record and led his team to a 20-14 record his senior year, as well as a third-place finish in the Catholic League—the school's best finish at the time (they even split with Poly).

Bond never made it to the NBA, but he couldn't have had a better prep and collegiate career. He went on to start at Stanford for three years, averaging 13.9 points per game. He went on to a career in the California State Assembly before passing away in 2005.

Shortly after Bond left for Palo Alto, Jack Errion rode into town and would coach the Saints to two decades of relevance from 1954 to 1975.

Jack Errion

Jack Errion got the St. Anthony job at just twenty-eight years old and quickly set about becoming an integral part of the Saints' campus. "He was a do-all guy. He coached football as well," says Walsh.

Errion took over a Saints program that had never won a league title and managed such a tightly run team that he often drove the bus himself over the twenty-two seasons he coached there. Known as a strict taskmaster, Errion coached an aggressive man defense that brought new energy and passion to the team. He was known to refer to the zone defense as "un-American."

BASKETBALL IN LONG BEACH

Jack Errion, legendary basketball coach for the Saints. The team's gym is named in his honor. *St. Anthony yearbook.*

"From what I've heard, he was a hard ass who really cared about his athletes," says Walsh.

Of course, change didn't happen overnight, but it took Errion only two years to bring a sub-.500 team all the way to the top, winning the Saints' first Catholic League title in 1956. No St. Anthony team had ever finished higher than third at that point, but Jim Senske and Jim Stephens helped lead the way.

BASKETBALL IN LONG BEACH

In those years, there was only one CIF division, which meant that St. Anthony was competing with the biggest schools in Southern California. Still, Errion led it to eleven league championships, an average of one every two years during his tenure, after the school started out with a thirty-six-year drought.

Because he was going up against the big powerhouses, Errion never captured a CIF championship while at the school. In fact, St. Anthony was routinely eliminated by other Long Beach schools, as Wilson and Jordan would both knock the Saints out of the playoffs.

The Saints' gym in those days was an absolute scene. It was hot, loud and smelly, with White Stags' fans seated right up next to the court on all four sides like a scene from *Hoosiers*. "There's nothing like that gym," says Long Beach basketball guru Frank Burlison. "Especially when you had good teams playing there."

After the activity he brought to the gym, it was fitting that the school would rename the facility the Jack Errion Gymnasium when he left.

Errion went on to a successful career at Corona del Mar, which he led to two CIF championships before unexpectedly passing away at the age of sixty-four in 1990.

BASKETBALL ON PARADE

One unique and special St. Anthony tradition that Errion started is Basketball on Parade, also known to generations of Saints alumni as BOP. A kind of hard court counterpoint to football's homecoming celebration, BOP has served as a school-wide celebration of the Saints' basketball teams and student body.

"I think that event is why we've kind of always been a basketball school," says Walsh. "It really built pride around basketball and elevated it to a level comparable to football on our campus."

The BOP celebrations have changed over the decades, and in recent years, they've included a week full of dress-up days with different themes. One constant is that they've allowed Saints students to get a look at the school's basketball teams, which have given them so many reasons to cheer over the years.

BASKETBALL IN LONG BEACH

Darrick Martin

No single Saints player has given St. Anthony fans more cause to cheer than Darrick Martin, the best St. Anthony basketball player ever and one of the most successful hoops athletes to come out of any school in the city.

Martin starred during the mid-1980s, graduating in 1988 after an accomplished prep career that saw him named McDonald's and PARADE All-American. Martin led the Saints on CIF playoff runs his sophomore and junior years. "Every time they had a home game, the gym was packed," says Walsh.

"Oh, it was crazy back then," remembers Martin. "You would never have believed we were a Catholic school. Mike McBride was the leader of the student section in the Pit, and he could get it going like no other. It was a great place to play—if we got you at home, we were up by eight points before we ran out of the tunnel."

Darrick Martin during his time at UCLA. Martin is the finest player ever for the Saints, and they recently renamed their court after him. Press-Telegram *file photo.*

Martin went on to UCLA and then a fifteen-year professional career that included thirteen years in the NBA. "In hindsight, that was the longest NBA career of any LB player," says

BASKETBALL IN LONG BEACH

Burlison of the five-eleven point guard with the silky-smooth jumper. Martin also played for a year with the Harlem Globetrotters. He retired in 2009 and has been coaching or working in an NBA front office since.

Martin is the pride of St. Anthony, not just because he's an alum who went on to great heights, but also because he maintained a close relationship with his alma mater. At UCLA and in the NBA, he wore St. Anthony gear under his uniform. Whenever he's in town, he still comes by Errion Gym to get some shots up.

"Brian sends me new gear every year so I can wear my St. Anthony stuff with pride," says Martin. "It's a very special place for me. I maintained a lot of friends from those years. I still get chills anytime I'm in town and I drive by the school."

The affection is mutual. A few years ago, the school renamed the floor at Errion Gym in Martin's honor.

THE CIF YEARS

The school did break through and finally get to hoist a CIF plaque; in fact, at the end of the 1999–2000 season, the Saints did it twice as the boys' and girls' teams both won their first championships in program history that year.

The boys, coached by Joe Luyben, defeated Pac Hills in the semifinals on a late bucket from Pearson Smith and went on to beat Calvary Chapel in the championship, 61–57, with Smith earning co–CIF Player of the Year honors.

The girls made the playoffs that year as a wild card and went on an improbable run, beating Avalon, Calvary Chapel (by forty points) and Buckley in the early rounds. They blew out Lone Pine in the quarterfinals and beat Chadwick in the semifinals, setting up a showdown with Pac Hills in the championship. The Saints, led by coach Eric Thorson, were ready. They jumped out to a 21–0 lead and went on to smash Pac Hills 65–34 in a game played in the Pyramid. Andrea Opfer earned CIF Player of the Year honors, leading a quality team with talents like Lisa Luyben and Starr Guillory.

The girls weren't done, however. Head coach James Anderson was hired to great acclaim and was expected to contend for championships. He did just that and won CIF titles in 2010 and 2011, beating Montclair Prep and Oaks Christian for the right to take home the golden plaque.

BASKETBALL IN LONG BEACH

The Saints girls' team went a step further than the boys, however, bringing home the state championship in Division V in 2011, beating Pinewood 62–44. Anderson's teams featured plenty of talent, but one genuine superstar was McDonald's All-American Kendall Cooper, who was a freshman and a sophomore on the two Saints championship teams.

Cooper was a consensus top fifteen recruit in the nation and one of the best female players to ever come out of Long Beach, signing with Duke out of high school. Named CIF Player of the Year after her sophomore season, Cooper continued to develop and play at a high level as a junior and senior, although the Saints teams weren't good enough to repeat their championship success.

Kendall Cooper, the best girls' player to come out of St. Anthony. *Courtesy St. Anthony.*

Cooper, a six-four post player who could also shoot the ball, closed out her career with the Saints in a playoff loss in one of the most impressive individual efforts by any prep LB player—she had twenty-five points, nineteen rebounds and thirteen blocks. She and Martin are the school's only McDonald's All-Americans.

For ninety years, St. Anthony has been known as Long Beach's little team that could. And with firm traditions in place and talented players always on the horizon, it's likely to remain that way for a long time to come.

10
MILLIKAN AND LAKEWOOD

Millikan and Lakewood High are forever intertwined, although their fan bases may not prefer it that way. Located just two miles apart and opened just one year apart—Millikan in 1956 and Lakewood in 1957—the two schools were actually built off the same blueprint so the Long Beach Unified School District could save on building costs.

That doesn't mean that the Rams and Lancers get along, of course. The two schools have enjoyed a healthy rivalry in several sports over the years. But that also doesn't mean that Long Beach's "suburban" schools aren't linked. Most notably, once Lakewood opened in the fall of 1957, there were enough schools in the Long Beach district that they could form their own athletic league, and the Moore League was officially born that fall.

MILLIKAN

The Rams have won three CIF championships, two by their boys' team and one from the girls. The successful runs for those Rams teams were spurred by strong, values-minded coaches who enjoyed long tenures with the team: Howard Lyon, Bill Odell and Lorene Morgan.

The school opened in 1956 and brought 2,600 students onto the newly minted campus over its first three years. Millikan was built at a cost of $6 million, and the first yearbooks printed there feature photographs of young students wandering campus, marveling at the pristine buildings.

The first basketball team the Rams put on the court was coached by "Red" Montgomery in 1957, a squad that went 17-9 and made the CIF playoffs in its inaugural year, losing to Newport Harbor. But Stan Anderson was named to the All-City team, and a first-year playoff appearance was certainly impressive.

The next year, the team was coached by Bob Hunt, and Anderson would win All-City Player of the Year by leading his team to the playoffs again with an 18-8 record. But it was the following season when the team began to take off with the hiring of Howard Lyon.

The Lyon's Roar

Lyon coached the Rams from 1959 to 1971, winning the school's first two league titles in '62–'63 and '69–'70. "Howie was just a great Christian man who ran a fantastic program," says his successor, Bill Odell.

Lyon was a lifelong Long Beach resident and loyal to the city through and through. A Poly grad, he went on to play at LBCC and then was captain on the first 49er basketball team at Long Beach State. After graduating from college with his degree and a teaching credential, Lyon dedicated himself to coaching Long Beach youth, spending a short time at Avalon High on Catalina Island before returning to his alma mater, where he coached for three years.

After that, he got the head job at Millikan and put his stamp on the program over the next twelve years. All told, his high school record was 325-133, or 71 percent wins. A devout Christian, he was offered the Biola job in the late 1960s but turned it down; he later told the *LA Times* he didn't think he was ready yet.

But after he coached a state all-star team—a group that included Jamaal Wilkes—he decided he wanted the challenge. "I had a pretty good thing going at Millikan," he told the *Times*. "About the best situation you could ask for as a coach."

Lyons also told the *Times* that the opportunity to coach at a religious school meant a lot. "The way I look at [life], you will either be with the Lord eternally or with the devil. I figured there are a lot of athletes out there that want to grow spiritually as well as in basketball, and I felt I could contribute to Biola having a strong program."

BASKETBALL IN LONG BEACH

He certainly did that, coaching there for eighteen years and posting a 409-163 record, leading the school to a 1984 NCCAA championship and to a national championship runner-up NAIA season in 1982 with a 39-1 record. He was also president of the NAIA Coaches Association at that time, while earning induction to the Long Beach Century Club, Long Beach State and SCIBCA Halls of Fame.

After retiring from Biola, Lyon continued to make his mark with Long Beach youth, serving as the Moore League secretary for more than a decade while helping to build up Long Beach's famous middle school sports program. The Rams named their gym in his honor after his passing in 2002.

Lyon coached plenty of great players in his 2-3 transitional zone defense while at Millikan, including future NFL player Gary Garrison, who was a football star at the school. But Millikan was more a basketball school in those years, thanks largely to Lyon's hardworking, entertaining teams. None is more fondly remembered than his 1970 championship team, which starred Dave Frost, who earned CIF Player of the Year honors and went on to play both basketball and baseball at LBCC and Stanford before enjoying a pro career on the diamond.

Millikan's 1970 CIF championship team. *Millikan yearbook.*

BASKETBALL IN LONG BEACH

Howard Lyon is carried off the court after the 1970 title game. The Rams' gym is named in his honor. *Millikan archive.*

Frost led a talented group that included All-CIF players Dan Peters and Richard Plante.

The Rams went 9-1 in the league with a loss to Wilson but still claimed the Moore League title. In the playoffs, they beat Dominguez, posted a seventeen-point fourth-quarter comeback against Pioneer and then beat Sunny Hills and handed Santa Barbara its first loss of the season to reach the championship. The Rams simply overwhelmed Monrovia in the title game, held at the LA Sports Arena. They won 68–37, the second-most lopsided CIF title game at that time and the first year a Long Beach team not named Poly won the title.

The Millikan teams of that era were made up of talented area kids who had great community pride and often starred for the Rams in multiple sports. For example, Garrison went on to a pro football career, and both Frost and Peters are members of the Long Beach Baseball Hall of Fame. Peters even came back to coach baseball at the school for a number of years, winning back-to-back CIF titles in 1991 and '92.

BASKETBALL IN LONG BEACH

Bill Odell

After Lyon departed for Biola, it was Bill Odell's turn to take over at Millikan. Odell had known Lyon for a while and respected him deeply—but there were some changes to be made.

"It was an interesting thing about Howie; he didn't coach during the summers," says Odell. "So Joe Romo would coach for the summer. When I got hired, I had to coach the summer. I couldn't not do it."

Odell had been coaching in West Covina for the three years prior to getting the Millikan job, so he wasn't as much of a known entity as most of the coaches working in Long Beach at the time. Lyon had been successful, but Odell had his own way. He changed Millikan's transitional zone defense to a more aggressive man approach.

"The thing that was important for me was that I inherited guys that hadn't played a lot of varsity, but we still won the league my first year," he says. "That set the bar that Howie is gone now, but we're still OK. We can handle this. When you take the place of someone so well known, that's helpful."

Odell certainly created his own legacy at Millikan, winning eight of the school's league titles in the twenty years he coached the Rams. They haven't won one since he departed. He also went to four championship games, playing in a time when the Moore League absolutely dominated the Southern California basketball scene.

"There was a sense in the city of it being special," he says. "You look back and it was amazing. There were lots of athletes, but it was a coaches' league. Not only were guys good coaches, but they were developing programs. They were the important figures. There wasn't an AAU guy around."

Odell says his best team was probably his '76–'77 squad, which wasn't one of his four CIF finalists. But that was a special year, probably the height of the Moore League basketball era, with three of the four semifinalists coming out of the league.

Bill Odell, the coach who won the Rams' second CIF title. *Millikan yearbook*.

BASKETBALL IN LONG BEACH

His first trip to the CIF finals was early in his career, in '73–'74, when the Jeff McHugh–led Rams fell to a stacked Verbum Dei team after entering the fourth quarter tied. The team that year upset Fountain Valley and Dominguez and then beat top-seeded Palos Verdes to make the finals.

"That was the beginning of some different things for me," says Odell.

It was a different experience for the Rams, as well, who had been competitive under Lyon but weren't a perennial powerhouse the way they would be in the '80s under Odell. Three of his last five years coaching there, they played for the CIF championship.

After what must have seemed an impossibly long wait, Odell finally won his championship on his third try in 1989. The Rams entered the league that year with a 14-2 record but dropped their first two league games to Lakewood and Poly.

"It was a real solid team that was tough," says Odell. "It wasn't my most talented team by any stretch of the imagination, but they did the right things and ended up winning it."

The Rams were heavy underdogs going into the championship game against Saddleback but were led by Arcadia transfer Jeep Jensen and Terry Hilliard. Jensen finally gave the Rams the last lead of the game on a runner late in overtime to give him twenty-one points, while center Demetrius Mayhand had fifteen points and grabbed ten rebounds. Millikan won 62–59 in overtime, completing what the *LA Times* and *Press-Telegram* called a "fairy tale–like finish."

"That's what you dream about, winning a CIF championship," says Odell. "When you've been there and haven't done it, you think about it a little bit more. That wasn't the reason I was coaching, but it was a good reward."

After that 1990–91 season, Odell followed Lyon's path and moved on, taking the job at Azusa Pacific. "That wasn't something I'd dreamed about, but Howie had great success moving on, and at that point my kids were in college and I could make a change and feel pretty good about it. To go to a Christian college was exciting, although it was hard to leave Millikan—but it was a good move for me."

That's an understatement. Odell took the Cougars, who had never won a conference title and had made the NAIA Tournament just once, and turned them into a national powerhouse. They won thirteen conference titles, including a record-setting nine in a row, and made the tournament fourteen times, including making the school's first-ever NAIA championship game. He retired in 2006 having won more games in a fifteen-year period than any NAIA coach ever—and he was inducted into the NAIA Hall of Fame in 2011.

BASKETBALL IN LONG BEACH

Lorene Morgan

But despite the success of the Millikan boys' teams, there was not much tradition of Rams girls' teams winning championships at Millikan, at least not for the first half of the school's existence. In 1989, the Rams hired Lorene Morgan to be their head coach, and she changed the culture from the ground up.

Prior to Morgan's hiring, the Rams had won only one league title and made the playoffs just a single time. Morgan has won five Moore League championships and a CIF championship, and her teams haven't missed the playoffs.

It's fortunate for Millikan fans that another Long Beach coaching great brought Morgan down from Washington, where she went to high school. Long Beach State's Joan Bonvicini recruited her. She didn't end up making a big dent in terms of the LBSU team, but she can be forgiven.

"Oh, I didn't do a lot of playing. I sat right behind LaTaunya Pollard," Morgan laughs, referring to the 49ers' best-ever player and winner of the Wade Trophy, given to the best player in the nation.

After Morgan graduated from Long Beach State, she worked for the Long Beach Parks & Recreation Department, becoming well known among the city's youth players while she ran the girls' sports program at Pan-Am Park. The result was that when she got the Millikan job, the talent level rose immediately. Her first teams featured All-CIF twins Tiffany and Taffany Maxwell, and she had the good fortune of coaching Nickey Hilbert, who went on to have a nice playing career at UCLA.

Lorene Morgan, the best girls' coach in Millikan history, was approaching five hundred wins in 2015. Morgan won all of Millikan's girls' league titles and its only CIF championship in 2014. *Photo courtesy Thomas Cordova.*

BASKETBALL IN LONG BEACH

Between Morgan's attention to detail as a coach and the increased talent level, the program flourished, and Morgan got to coach several special talents, including Courtney Clements, who went on to San Diego State and then became the first Long Beach hoopster to make the WNBA when she debuted with the Atlanta Dream. Clements helped lead Millikan to the CIF championship game in 2008, when they fell to league rival Poly in the Pyramid at Long Beach State.

A very good career became a great career in 2014, when Morgan's Rams pushed her over the top and claimed the school's first girls' basketball CIF title. They were a talented and versatile team that featured Alyssa Benton, named CIF Player of the Year, and Briana Guillory, All-CIF. The Rams beat Bonita 56–53 to claim the championship.

"Without a doubt, I think my career would have felt incomplete without it," Morgan says. "That's a goal we have every year, and it's something that's been in front of us."

Morgan was approached by former players who joked that they deserved rings, too, for helping build the program.

"It was something I needed to get done, for me and for them," Morgan says. "Sending kids to college, graduating them—that's the important stuff. But in our community, you have to raise the plaque to legitimize things. The banner is in the gym. It's happened now, it's there. It sets the bar for the future."

Lakewood

It's never smart to take sides in a rivalry, but it's fair to say that Millikan has been the better basketball program over the school's history than Lakewood. The Lancers have nonetheless had some genuine high points, however. Both the boys' and girls' teams have won three league titles, five of them shared with at least one other team. The Lancer boys' and girls' teams each have one league title as part of a three-way tie for the crown, representing the only two times that's happened in Moore League history.

The peak for the Lakewood boys' program came during Tim Sweeney's run at the school; he coached the Lancers from 1980 until his resignation in 1992. Sweeney won two league titles, sharing it with Millikan and Poly in 1982 and with Millikan in 1989.

Sweeney was a Poly grad who played on the Jackrabbits' 1960 championship team under Bill Mulligan, and he knew early in life that

BASKETBALL IN LONG BEACH

he wanted to coach. After playing at Chapman College, he immediately jumped into the coaching ranks at Mount SAC, where he was an assistant.

He coached lower level at Lakewood and at his alma mater, hoping to get the head job when it opened up, but the school opted for Ron Palmer, and Sweeney ended up coaching JV at Lakewood and then assisting at Chapman until the Lancers' job finally became available. His story illustrates the depth and quality of Long Beach's coaches in that era. It's amazing that a man of that caliber could essentially spend eight years working his way up in the coaching minor leagues of Long Beach before finally getting a Moore League varsity head job.

"Younger coaches today are not being mentored in that way," says Sweeney. "I had to wait eight years. I was passed over at Poly, which really disappointed me. I was brought into the school district to be a head coach and had to wait and work for it. I think that made me a better coach."

Sweeney was able to change the culture at Lakewood and get better athletes into the school very quickly. "We knew we had to change the culture because it had always been a baseball/football school," he says. "What helped us out early on was that I did go to Poly and I was close with people in that community. I think there was a degree of trust from people, even though Lakewood didn't exactly welcome desegregation with open arms."

Although he coached there in the 1980s, Sweeney actually coached the Lancers' first African American players. But with his local ties and the fact that Poly's legendary coach Ron Palmer was at Long Beach State for part of Sweeney's run, he was able to get kids to Lakewood who wouldn't normally have gone there.

"He was getting guys from North Long Beach and the Eastside because they trusted him," says Long Beach basketball guru Frank Burlison.

Sweeney certainly proved himself in the 1981–82 season, when he captured the Lancers' first Moore League title and its first CIF championship to boot with one of the Moore League's all-time greatest teams. "That was a hell of a team," says Burlison. "That might be the best non–Ron Palmer Poly team that I saw in Long Beach."

After tying for the league title, Lakewood made a run through the playoffs, beating Ocean View and then a Rolling Hills team that featured Jay Bilas in the quarterfinals. CIF Player of the Year Tod Murphy led a skilled team that featured Barry Barnes and Dwayne Corbett, whose brother had starred at Jordan.

In a championship game played downtown at the Long Beach Arena, the Lancers defeated Inglewood 82–70.

BASKETBALL IN LONG BEACH

Murphy played college ball at UC Irvine and then went on to a twelve-year pro career after being drafted by the Seattle Supersonics. His career included five years in the NBA with the Clippers, Timberwolves, Pistons and Warriors. Murphy went into coaching shortly after retiring from playing in Japan and is currently the head coach at Gordon College.

Sweeney coached other great players while at Lakewood, including Duane Cooper, who was drafted by the Lakers out of USC. Sweeney's run came to an end in 1992 after a controversial incident. Sweeney was suspended by the Moore League for most of the 1992–93 season for a recruiting violation. He gave a handwritten note to eighth-grade Ortege Jenkins, an excellent player who lived in the Jordan district. Panthers coach Ron Massey sent a copy of the note to the CIF Southern Section, and the Moore League principals voted to suspend Sweeney for the non-league portion of the next season, as well as the first round of league play.

"I was just disappointed in that I never got any representation or say. They just handed down the edict," says Sweeney, who said at the time that the note was simply a congratulatory message to Jenkins for winning the All-City middle school championship with Hoover. "In my opinion, there were a few people in the district in power positions that didn't like the fact that we were successful and didn't like that there were players leaving to come over with us."

Time has healed all wounds. Sweeney says he carries no bitterness about the incident, and the school welcomed him back in 2010 for a renaming ceremony in which it dedicated the gym in his name. "I have no hard feelings or regrets," he says. "My memories go back to the great players I've coached. They graduated, they're working—I love following them."

He'll have a great chance to follow one of those players, as Cooper was hired by Lakewood shortly before this book went to print to be the Lancers' new head coach. He replaces Matt Ruiz, a former Long Beach State women's basketball assistant who went on to coach the Lancers for twenty years, winning Lakewood's last league title in 2005 with a team led by Leon Young, Brandon Nevens and Patrick Rembert.

INDEX

A

Allen Field House 49
Amateur Athletic Union (AAU) 24, 71
Amberry, Tom 121
American Basketball Association (ABA) 73–74
American Basketball League (ABL) 71–72, 74–76
Anderson, Gary 40, 42, 117, 124–126, 127–128
Anderson, Larry 56–57

B

Bartow, Guy 81
Basketball on Parade 153–155
Big West
  Conference 47, 51
  Freshman of the Year 49, 52, 56
  Player of the Year 53, 56–57
  Tournament 48, 50, 52, 54, 56
Bola, Dallas 68
Bond, Bill 151
Bonvicini, Joan 61–63, 64–68, 139, 163
Boston Celtics 28, 42, 133
Brightman, Al 72, 133–135
Brown, Cindy 64, 66
Bryant, Kobe 77
Bryant, Travon 145
Buggs, Carl 90, 111–115
Burlison, Frank 34, 48, 50, 53, 69–70, 96, 98, 100, 102, 106, 110, 116, 143, 146, 153, 155, 165

C

California Collegiate Athletic Association (CCAA) 16
California Junior College Player of the Year 20, 21, 27, 125, 143
Carr, Vance 24–25
Cegles, Vic 68
Church, Charlie 17, 46, 89–91, 110, 117, 121–123, 126
CIF championship 79–80, 88, 90–91, 102–103, 105–106, 110–111, 113, 116, 139–140, 145–146, 150, 153, 157, 162–164
Clear, Paula 139–140
Coffin, Roy 81
Columbus Quest 75
Comer, Dr. Lew 39
Compton 29, 36, 83, 91–92, 94, 118, 120–121, 124, 126, 131–132, 137

INDEX

Compton Junior College 16, 44
Cooper, Kendall 156
Cotton, James 52
Crilley, Elizabeth 128–129
Cutler, Kevin 48

D

Dallas Mavericks 50
Davis-Wrightstil, Clarissa 75
Dayman, Esther 85
DeRozan, DeMar 78
Dial, Derrick 73
Diggs, AJ 105–106
Diggs, Shelton 105, 109–110
Dingman, Mae 83
Drew League 78
Driesell, Lefty 47
Duncan, Ivan 25
Durant, Kevin 78

E

Edney, Tyus 103, 108, 110
Elite Eight 44, 47, 53, 55, 66
Ennis, James 57
Errion, Jack 151–153

F

Fab Four 56–57
Ferguson, Jim 70, 124, 138
Final Four 18, 38, 41, 44, 47, 64, 66–67, 69, 123, 127, 139
Fisher, Derek 77
Florentine, Bill 17–18
Frazer, Fred 131, 133, 135
Fresno State 16, 19, 21
Frost, Dave 159–160

G

Gambril, Don 19
Garnett, Kevin 77
Gervin, George 33–34
Girls' Athletic Association 85–88
Gold Mine 33, 52, 63, 66

Gonzaga 55
Gray, Leonard 33, 39, 42
Greenberg, Seth 46–47, 49, 51–53
Griffin, Melvin 119–120
Griffith, Yolanda 75
Gritton, Ray 36
Gross, Bob 40, 42
Gwynn, Tony 98, 110

H

Hardy, James 141, 143
Harlem Globetrotters 71, 76, 155
Harrington, Joe 47–49, 53
Harris, Lucious 48, 50–52
Haywood, Spencer 34–35, 73
Hegarty, Mary 68
Houston Rockets 39
Howard, Bob 90, 110–111, 120, 136, 157

I

Idaho 43, 54–55, 134

J

Jefferson High 20
Johnson, Kejuan 54
Johnson, Magic 76
Jones, Dave 17–18, 121
Jones, Dwight 42, 44

K

Kansas 50, 56, 73, 115
Kansas State 15, 27, 30, 39, 44, 48
Kidd, Earl 16–17
Kienholz, Ed 82, 88–89
Kim, Art 72
Kingcade, Lily 83

L

Lacy, Venus 75
Lakers 34, 45, 72, 76–77, 134, 166
Landreth, Orian "Todd" 89
Leslie, Lisa 66–67

INDEX

Lewis, Raymond 36–37
Lindahl, Lorie 61, 147
Llewelyn, Clarinne 87
Long Beach Arena 37–38, 70, 98, 165
Long Beach Breakers 74
Long Beach Century Club 135, 159
Long Beach Chiefs 71–72, 135
Long Beach City College 15, 17–19, 25, 27, 38, 40, 46, 117–129, 137, 138
Long Beach Elks 71
Long Beach Jam 73–74
Long Beach Press-Telegram 19, 34, 38, 53, 69, 76, 80, 93, 143, 162
Long Beach Stingrays 74–76
Long Beach Storm 74
Lyon, Howard 93, 157–160, 161–162

M

Marquette 37, 44
Martin, Darrick 154–155
Massey, Ron 143–147, 166
McCormack, Jim 19, 30
McDonald, Glenn 28, 34, 39–40, 42, 68
McGrady, Tracy 77
McHugh, Maura 74–76
McMillian, Lloyd 42–43
Metoyer, Sharrief 103, 105–110, 127
Middough, Hazel 86
Middough, Lorne 81
Middough, Way 82, 89
Milisa, Mate 53
Miller, Dr. Fred 19
Mina, Carlos 40, 42
Mohr, Margaret 66, 139
Monson, Dan 53–57
Montgomery, Dr. Jack 16
Montgomery, Mike 18
Moore League 70, 88, 91, 94, 96, 98, 102, 109–111, 113, 131, 135–144, 147, 157, 159–161, 163–166
Morgan, J.D. 29, 37

Morgan, Lorene 157, 163–164
Morgan, Wayne 53

N

Naismith Memorial Basketball Hall of Fame 33, 38, 42, 123, 134
National Invitation Tournament (NIT) 21, 47, 49, 55, 68, 134
NCAA
 probation 39, 40, 42, 44, 54
 Tournament 21, 25, 27, 42, 50, 52, 55–57, 62, 66–67, 72, 99, 103, 134
Nixon, Aaron 54

O

Odell, Bill 70, 157–158, 161–162
Olson, Lute 27, 38–42, 44, 49, 117, 123–126, 127
Olympics 18, 37, 66, 87, 90, 129

P

Pacific Coast Athletic Association (PCAA) 21, 27, 33, 37, 40, 42–44
Palmer, Ron 47, 53, 70, 90, 96–105, 106, 108–110, 147, 165
Palmgren, Ben 141–143
Pasadena City College 19, 24
Patterson, Bill 16, 136–137
Perry, Richard 16–18, 62, 136–137
Phelps, Eugene 56
Pollard, LaTaunya 62–63, 66, 163
"Poly Way, the" 105, 110, 116
Pondexter, Clifton 41–42
Pondexter, Roscoe 39–41
Prince, Roschon 106–110
Prindle, Donna 128–129

R

Rambo, John 17–18, 94
Ratleff, Ed 22, 23–27, 28, 33–34, 37, 39, 45–46, 52, 56
Reynolds, Larry 53–54, 55

INDEX

Riverside City College 19
Robinson, Jean 85
Robinson, Sam 20–22
Robinson, T.J. 56
Rocha, Red 72
Rodman, Dennis 73
Rosborough, Joel 144–146, 147
Russell, Bryon 50, 52

S

Sandefur, Randy 18
Saperstein, Abe 71–72, 134
Sapriel, Daniella 129
Schaafsma, Dr. Frances 59–61, 62
Schwarzkopf, Herm 15–16
Seattle University 61, 72, 133, 135
Smith, Bert 117–119
SoCal title 84
Southern California Catholic Girls' Basketball Tournament 149
South Florida 52–53
Stangeland, Jim 19
Steinbrenner, George 72
Stoudemire, Amare 77
Summitt, Pat 64, 66
Sweeney, Tim 70, 102, 164–166

T

Tarkanian, Jerry 19–22, 24–25, 28, 30–40, 42, 44, 46, 50, 52, 57, 91
Taylor, Mina 83
Terry, Chuck 27–28, 33, 36, 125, 143
Tinklepaugh, Verna 84–85
Title IX 59, 88, 110, 128, 150
Toler, Penny 64, 66
Trapp, George 21–22, 27–28, 30–32, 34, 46, 56

U

UCLA 16, 20–21, 27–32, 33, 36–37, 39, 42, 54, 61, 66–67, 76, 103, 112–113, 115, 134, 138, 142, 154–155, 163

University of Iowa 41
UNLV 37, 38, 44, 46, 52, 62, 113, 115, 139
Upton, Gertrude 82–85

W

Walker, Del 90–93, 110, 123–124
Wall, John 78
Walter Pyramid 52, 73–74, 77, 139
Walton, Bill 33, 42, 138
Ware, Casper 56–57
Watson, Martha 87
Western Regional
 Finals 33
 semifinals 21
Wicks, Sidney 21, 29, 33
Wiley, Michael 42–44, 46–47, 97–98, 110
Wiley, Morlon 47, 101–102, 110
Wilkerson, Dana 66
Winter, Tex 39, 42–46
Women's Basketball League of Southern California 83
Women's National Basketball Association (WNBA) 66, 74–75, 164
Wooden, John 21, 28, 30, 36, 72, 96, 102, 134–135, 138, 142
Wynn, Jody 68

About the Authors

Mike Guardabascio was born and raised in Long Beach, California. He has been writing professionally for twelve years and has been published in over two dozen magazines and newspapers. For the last seven years, he's been a sportswriter covering high school and college sports in Long Beach as co-editor of the *Grunion Gazette* sports section and co-prep sports editor of the *Press-Telegram*. He is the author of a previous book from The History Press, *Football in Long Beach*. He lives in Long Beach with his wife, Shar, and their son, Vincent. He can be reached via e-mail at mike.guardabascio@presstelegram.com.

Chris Trevino was born and raised in Laurel, Maryland. He is a 2013 graduate of the University of Maryland, College Park. Chris has been writing about sports for five years, having been published in the *Baltimore Sun* and *Washington Post*. On a fall

ABOUT THE AUTHORS

morning in 2013, Chris packed up his Jeep and drove across the country (in three days) to join the *Long Beach Press-Telegram* as a sportswriter. He lives in Long Beach and can be reached via e-mail at christian.trevino@presstelegram.com.